How I wish I had had this book forty-one years ago when I was ordained a deacon! The books I read at that time had what I (even then) suspected to be an unbiblical footing. Webb gives a thorough history of earlier ideas that were erroneous about the diaconate (I read some of the books at the time) and then gives biblical citations (including discussions of the Greek words that laymen can understand) of the true role of the deacon as taught and practiced in the Bible. This book is full of practical suggestions that should make selection and ordination a much easier job for churches. It is a guidebook for deacons themselves that is thoroughly biblical. It has a large number of sensible and realistic suggestions that I hope my church will apply (for example, the deacon's *real* examination should precede the actual ordination day). Most important, this book shows why the deacon is a true servant leader and cannot function in that role without a genuine walk with God—the main emphasis the Bible itself places on the deacon's daily walk. Every deacon should study this book thoroughly—and I think every pastor and church leader should too!

T. W. Hunt
Author, *The Mind of Christ*

Here is a Bible-based guidebook for deacons and leaders in the church. My good friend, Henry Webb, has thoroughly researched his subject, has corrected past misnomers of some authors, and has rendered a comprehensive and practical approach to the vital ministry of Christian leadership in the church. It is my prayer that God will use this book for His glory and the enrichment of local churches everywhere.

Stephen F. Olford, Founder and Senior Lecturer
The Stephen Olford Center for Biblical Preaching
Memphis, Tennessee

Henry Webb has made a significant contribution to the ministry of local churches with his recently released book *Deacons: Servant Models in the Church*. It is extremely well written, easy to read, and faithful to the Scriptures. Pastors and churches would be wise to place this book into the hands of all of their deacons—especially those who are newly ordained. It is an invaluable tool!

Junior Hill, Evangelist

Without doubt, the role of deacons in our churches is a matter of utmost importance. Good, functioning deacons who protect the fellowship of the church and serve the church with humility is one of the greatest needs today. Henry Webb has skillfully written about the place of deacons and their role as servant models in the church. These pages will help to solidify the biblical ministry of the deacons and encourage deacons to serve in the spirit of Christ and the church to appropriately respond to that ministry.

James T. Draper Jr., President
LifeWay Christian Resources

Henry Webb has captured the spirit of the New Testament deacon with amazing clarity. The church is in desperate need for great leaders. God's Word clearly states that to be great we must become servants. The perfect model of the deacon is a selfless servant leader. *Deacons: Servant Models in the Church* is a model textbook for every pastor and every deacon.

Bob Reccord, President
North American Mission Board

This is a must-read book for anyone in the deacon ministry. It is thoroughly biblical, providing insight on the historical development of the deacon ministry plus a fresh view of what the deacon's role should be today. *Deacons: Servant Models in the Church* should be the foundational book to train every deacon.

Elgia "Jay" Wells, Director
Black Church Leadership, LifeWay Christian Resources

I have known Dr. Henry Webb as a friend and fellow servant of Jesus Christ for over forty years. Henry and I were college roommates, and I can say with confidence that Henry Webb openly models everything he suggests for pastors and deacons in his revised book, *Deacons: Servant Models in the Church*. I have personally enjoyed using his servant-model concept and have served on numerous deacon groups that have thrived using Henry's deacon plan. I commend Henry's creative service concept and recommend, without reservation, his book as an inspiring, practical, workable guide for individual deacons, deacon groups, and servant pastors.

Jerry R. Day, Deacon

It is my privilege to know Henry Webb as a friend, fellow deacon, and colaborer in Christ for over twenty years. Having served two times with him as a deacon officer, I know from firsthand experience the joy there is to "join in following his example." Henry doesn't just write about serving as a deacon, but is truly a servant model for deacons everywhere. Every church would profit from having this book as a study for all deacons.

Harris N. Scott III, Deacon

Deacons: Servant Models in the Church is right on target. It is biblically sound, historically accurate—and is filled with practical suggestions for strengthening deacon ministry.

Howard B. Foshee
Author, *Now That You're a Deacon*

This book by Henry Webb gives valuable information about how to serve in the role of deacon. His emphasis on servanthood as the model helps any deacon or deacon candidate to more fully understand the biblical role of a deacon. As such it is a valuable addition to the training materials available for deacons.

Bob Sheffield
Author, *The Ministry of Baptist Deacons*

Henry Webb provides a practical, biblically based model for deacon ministry. He tackles tough interpretive issues while pointing us in the right direction for deacon ministry for the future. This time-honored message is a must for everyone who serves as a deacon in the church.

Gene Wilkes
Author, *Jesus on Leadership*

As I read through the new version of *Deacons: Servant Models in the Church*, I thought of several appropriate words. *Timely, balanced, mature, useful,* and *challenging* were just some of the words. Henry Webb has given us an up-to-date training tool to use in preparing Christian laymen to serve as deacons in our churches. I'll look forward to using this book in the training of the deacons of First Baptist Church, Lubbock.

D. L. Lowrie, Pastor
First Baptist Church, Lubbock, Texas

Wow! We've needed this clear view of biblical expectations for deacons, ready to lead as servants, in both ministry and evangelism. A perfect fit to FAITH! Should be required reading for all who would serve as a deacon!

Bobby Welch, Senior Pastor
First Baptist Church, Daytona Beach, Florida

This first-rate book is the brightest and most research-oriented book on the ministry of a deacon, yet it is an easy read. From the biblical job description, Henry shows us how our lives weave together in ministry and covers completely the role of the deacon as a servant. I recommend this book as mandatory reading for all deacons and church staff.

Montia Setzler, Pastor
Magnolia Avenue Baptist Church, Riverside, California

Henry Webb's *Deacons: Servant Models in the Church* is an excellent introduction to the ministry of the deacon. He clarifies the necessity of character, answers many how-to questions, and makes numerous wise suggestions with respect to implementation. The best part of all, however, is that Henry models authentically what he counsels others to do. Every pastor and deacon needs to have this volume as a ready reference.

Jerry Sutton, Pastor
Two Rivers Baptist Church, Nashville, Tennessee

It is my joy to recommend to readers who love the church the new book by Henry Webb, *Deacons: Servant Models in the Church*. Henry's first book on the deacon was written several years ago and has been the model for thousands of deacons. This is an update of the book, and it will meet the needs of a new generation of readers.

Roy T. Edgemon
Coauthor, *The Ways of God*

One of the significant untapped resources in many churches is the deacons. This unrealized potential exists because congregations have failed to utilize deacons effectively and because deacons have failed to understand the biblical basis for their role. Both of these shortcomings can be overcome as congregations, pastors, and deacons study *Deacons: Servant Models in the Church*. A serious study and application of concepts developed in this book can result in deacons who function as ministering partners to the glory of God and for the strengthening of the churches.

C. Ferris Jordan, Emeritus Professor
New Orleans Baptist Theological Seminary

Deacons: Servant Models in the Church is an excellent source of information about biblical teachings and current church practices, a basic text for prospective deacons, current deacons, and all church members who desire to know how deacons help churches grow the kingdom of God. Dr. Webb acknowledges the variety of ways deacons may effectively serve churches, while keeping the emphasis squarely on the New Testament model of servant ministry. For more than thirty years I have observed his ministry to others and received with gratitude his ministry to my family.

Ernest E. Mosley
Author, *Priorities in Ministry*

DEACONS

DEACONS
Servant Models in the Church

❧ U P D A T E D   E D I T I O N ❧

HENRY WEBB

BROADMAN
&HOLMAN
PUBLISHERS

Nashville, Tennessee

0–8054–2463–6

Published by Broadman & Holman Publishers,
Nashville, Tennessee

Dewey Decimal Classification: 253
Subject Heading: DEACONS

Unless otherwise noted, Scripture quotations have been taken from the
Holman Christian Standard Bible, © 2000 by Holman Bible Publishers. Used
by permission. Quotations from other versions are marked as follows:
GNB, Good News Bible: The Bible in Today's English Version, © American
Bible Society 1966, 1971, 1976; used by permission. NASB, the New
American Standard Bible, © the Lockman Foundation, 1960, 1962, 1963,
1968, 1971, 1972, 1973, 1975, 1977; used by permission. NIV, the Holy
Bible, New International Version, copyright © 1973, 1978, 1984 by
International Bible Society.

Library of Congress Cataloging-in-Publication Data

Webb, Henry, 1937–
    Deacons : servant models in the church / Henry
        Webb.—Updated ed.
    p. cm.
    ISBN 0–8054–2463–6
    1. Deacons—Baptists. I. Title.

BX6346 .W35 2001
253—dc21
                                                    2001035749
            1 2 3 4 5 6 7 8 9 10 05 04 03 02 01

To my two sons
whom I love and who faithfully serve
their Lord, families, and churches.
Craig, as pastor
Chuck, as deacon

Contents

Preface

I am convinced that the ministry role of deacons as expressed in the New Testament is appropriate today. As a young pastor, I was grateful for Howard Foshee's guidance in *The Ministry of the Deacon* in clarifying the tasks of deacons. Through the years, I have been challenged and honored to be involved in continuing to express these New Testament principles and the practical application for deacon ministry as editor of *The Deacon,* leader in deacon conferences, as a deacon, and through the pages of this book.

The purpose of the first edition of this book released in 1980 was to help deacons to demonstrate in their lives and to apply in their churches the biblical concepts of their role as servant leaders. That purpose is unchanged in this updated edition. I am grateful to Broadman & Holman for giving this book life for future generations of deacons.

Chapter 1 guides the congregation to determine its procedures for selecting and ordaining deacons. A careful process can assure the electing and setting apart of those who will truly be servant models for the church. Chapters 2 through 5 explore the biblical qualifications for deacons. Deacons are expected to model growth toward mature faith, Christian family life, personal and public morality, and a life accepted by God and the church. The opportunity for deacons to model ministry as partners with the pastor is the focus of chapter 6. This includes the emerging role of deacons through the centuries and the organizing of deacons to minister to persons more effectively. The last three chapters suggest more specific ways deacons can carry out their responsibility to minister. As they respond to the needs of persons and the church, they can model care for families, proclamation of the gospel, and Christian leadership.

Many persons deserve praise for helping this book become reality:

- The members of Kalihi Baptist Church, Honolulu, Hawaii, trusted me to be their pastor for nearly nine years. They gave me support, freedom, and help to grow as a person and as a pastor.
- My ordination as a deacon by Two Rivers Baptist Church, Nashville, Tennessee, was a meaningful act of Christian encouragement. My fellow deacons in that church have demonstrated the principles of this book.
- Deacons in conferences I have led have excited me with their quality of commitment to Christ and their desire to be effective servants in their churches.
- I have been fortunate to be surrounded by people who have loved me and believed in me—wife and sons, daughters-in-law and grandchildren, parents and sisters, teachers and coworkers, church members and friends, pastors and deacons.
- My greatest thanks must go to my wife, Patti, for her constant moral support and her patience with me as I continue to grow as a Christian and husband.

I pray that God will use this book to encourage and help you fulfill the challenging task to be a servant model in your church. I am confident that these words of Paul will continue to be true of deacons in every generation. "Those who have served well as deacons acquire a good standing for themselves, and great boldness in the faith that is in Christ Jesus" (1 Tim. 3:13). May all be done to honor and glorify God and to accomplish his purpose.

—Henry Webb

CHAPTER I

The Church Needs Servant Models

ONE OF THE GREATEST COMPLIMENTS people can pay Christians is to view them as examples for other Christians to follow. Paul paid that compliment to the Christians in Thessalonica. "You became a model to all the believers . . . . Your faith in God has become known everywhere" (1 Thess. 1:7–8 NIV). Their pattern of Christian living was a model worthy of imitation by other Christians. They were living examples of the Christlike life.

The disciples were first called Christians in Antioch (Acts 11:26). Those who are called by Christ's name should be honored to model his life in their lives.

Paul encouraged Timothy to "be an example to the believers in speech, in conduct, in love, in faith, in purity" (1 Tim. 4:12). He also challenged Titus to "set them an example by doing what is good" (Titus 2:7 NIV).

The primary model for all Christians is Jesus Christ himself. He left "you an example, so that you should follow in His steps" (1 Pet. 2:21). Jesus came to serve. He said, "The Son of Man did not come to be served, but to serve, and to give his life—a ransom for many" (Mark 10:45).

Jesus dramatically illustrated his servant lifestyle for his disciples. He washed their feet at their last meal together before his arrest and crucifixion. He wanted them to learn unmistakably a basic lesson of servanthood. "Do you know what I have done for you? You call Me Teacher and Lord. This is well said, for I am. So if I, your Lord and Teacher, have washed your feet, you also ought to wash one another's feet. For I have given you an example that you also should do as I have done for you" (John 13:12–15).

All followers of Jesus are to serve by providing ministry in his name. The title *diakonos* (servant) applies to every Christian, but the apostle Paul also used it in a special sense for specific church leaders (Phil. 1:1; 1 Tim. 3:8–13). Translators chose not to translate literally in those situations but to make a new English word *deacon* from the Greek word for servant. Thus deacons carry both the name of Christ and the name of servant.

The high qualifications for the pastors (overseers) and deacons found in 1 Timothy 3 clearly indicate that the New Testament churches looked to these church leaders for examples in Christian living. This continues to be true in today's churches.

The congregation looks to its pastor and deacons to serve as models both in their quality of life and in their active ministry. This chapter guides the congregation to determine its procedures for selecting and ordaining deacons who truly will be servant models for the church.

Selecting Deacons for Ministry

The selection of deacons is one of the most important events in the life of a church. The process of choosing these spiritual leaders can be a meaningful experience for the congregation, for those chosen, and for their families. Careful planning and appropriate procedures can make that possible.

Churches use a variety of methods. Certainly there is no one right way to nominate and elect deacons. Some of the factors that influence the church's procedure are tradition, the size of the church, and the duties of the deacons. Churches need to select deacon nomination and election procedures that fit their needs. A church should use a method that will assure the election of deacons who are both biblically qualified and deeply committed to deacon ministry.

The most common denominator in churches is that the congregation votes to elect the deacons. However, the variables include such areas as (1) church-required qualifications (in addition to biblical qualifications), (2) term of service, (3) nomination and screening of candidates, and (4) preparation of the congregation for the selection process. The number of deacons needed is based on a balance between the number needed to carry out the deacon ministry and the number of those in the congregation who are qualified to serve.

Church-Required Qualifications

Most churches have some age requirement for deacons. The intent is that deacons should have broad enough adult experience to be able to minister maturely to a cross section of members. Of course, such maturity does not come to all persons at the same age. However, churches have most often set the minimum age at twenty-one.

Many churches also require prospective deacons to be church members for a specified period of time. This gives church members a more adequate opportunity to become familiar with their qualifications for deacon service. This time also gives prospective deacons an opportunity to become familiar with the nature and style of the church and how deacons minister in it. A one-year requirement is most common, but some churches require as little as six months and others as much as two years.

Churches often require some external signs of commitment to the church. Most frequently cited is regular participation in church programs such as Sunday school/Bible study, discipleship, Sunday worship services, and midweek prayer service. Deacons often also are expected to be tithers, giving 10 percent or more of their income through the church budget. A church may also require regular deacons' meeting attendance and participation in specific training for deacon ministry.

Other requirements usually derive from the biblical qualifications for deacons found in 1 Timothy 3:8–13 and for church leaders found in Acts 6:3. Chapters 2 through 5 explore these qualifications in detail.

Term of Service

Some churches continue to have deacons serve indefinitely on the active deacon body. These churches have deacon elections only when there are vacancies or the deacon body is enlarged. But many churches elect deacons for a limited period of time. Almost all the latter churches use a three-year term. However, some have chosen a four-year or other longer, specified term.

The phrase "rotation of deacons" means that the term of only a portion of the deacons expires each year. In most cases after serving the specified term, the deacon is ineligible for reelection for one year. Those elected to fill a vacancy for one year or less usually are eligible for reelection for a full term. Churches usually choose a rotation approach for two reasons: (1) This approach provides continuity with only a portion of the deacons rotating off the active body each year, and (2) this approach makes it possible for more members to serve as deacons. Reserve deacons who have rotated off the active body can continue to minister as servants through other church responsibilities. They may also help with some of the ministries assigned to deacons. They will be ready to assume the deacon role again if reelected by the church. Some churches use a three-year term but do not require the year off before reelection to another term.

Some churches confer the title of "deacon emeritus" in recognition and honor for long-standing deacon service. The term *emeritus* means that the deacon has retired from an active position, usually when no longer physically able to carry out the duties of an active deacon.

Nomination of Candidates

A widely used nominating procedure is nomination by the entire congregation. Churches generally use one of two approaches. Some distribute to every church member a ballot listing all eligible members. The members mark the names they want to nominate up to the number of vacancies to be filled. Other churches have a blank ballot for persons to list the names of individuals whom they feel are qualified for the role. Some churches use Sunday school classes or other small groups as a source for nominations.

Another method is nomination by committee. This committee is either a special committee that nominates only deacons or a church nominating committee that nominates other leaders as well. Either committee would need to study carefully the qualifications and duties of deacons.

In some churches the existing deacons nominate other deacons because they believe the deacons understand the work of deacons best. The strong disadvantage of this approach is that the deacons become a self-perpetuating group.

Screening of Candidates

One of the most important steps in selecting deacons is interviewing prospective nominees. The purpose of the interview is to determine if a person is qualified according to biblical and church requirements, understands and is committed to the ministry of the deacon, and is willing to serve if elected.

If the congregation nominates, the pastor and deacon chairman often do the interviewing. Sometimes other church staff members and deacon officers assist in this process. If a committee or the deacons nominate, that group or the pastor and deacon chairman may do the interviewing.

It is appropriate to have the prospective deacons' family present during the interview. The interviewers should be prepared to present thorough information about qualifications, the duties of deacons, and church expectations. Questioning should be in a positive spirit. The best questions are ones the candidate needs to answer in deciding whether to agree to be nominated. To avoid possible embarrassment, the personal interview should seek to cover anything that might be brought up later in an examination council.

If a church uses an examination council in addition to or instead of the more personal interviewing process, the council should be scheduled well in advance of the election and ordination service. Prospective deacons should still be informed of qualifications and expectations of a deacon. This could be in written form. Sometimes pastors and deacons from other Baptist churches in the area are also invited to participate in the examination council. The council should possess a positive spirit and never become an inquisition. Areas of inquiry would be the same as in the more personal screening.

Sometimes a period of training is also required before a nominee is presented to the congregation for election. The time period for the deacon selection will often be determined by how much time is needed for the screening process. Adequate time is essential.

Preparation of the Congregation

The congregation needs to be prepared adequately for the election of deacons. If the congregation nominates as well as elects, preparation should begin before the nomination. Biblical and church qualifications, the duties of deacons, and the selection procedure should be interpreted. This can be done through sermons, articles in the church newsletter, or churchwide training using this book.

Following the nominating and screening process, the nominating group will bring a list of nominees to the congregation for election. In some churches the number is the same as the number of vacancies to be filled. In other churches the list is larger, up to double the number of vacancies. If the latter plan is used, the list should include several more nominees than vacancies to be filled. This avoids the embarrassment of a single nominee not being elected.

Deacon nominees should be introduced to the congregation. To assume everyone knows them is a mistake. The pastor can introduce prospective deacons in a church service, or photographs and biographical sketches can be printed in a church bulletin or newsletter. Some churches provide a reception where members can meet and talk with nominees.

The election itself should be by a printed, secret ballot. This is often held on a Sunday morning to get the widest participation possible. Some churches make provisions for absentee voting. To announce the number of votes each person receives is unwise and unnecessary.

The entire selection process should be long enough to be orderly and efficient but not so long that church members get tired of the process. Once a church determines its selection procedure, it should record the process in detail in the church bylaws or in an official document on "Guidelines for Selection of Deacons."

Setting Deacons Apart for Ministry

The New Testament records surprisingly little about ordination. Churches often refer to the account of the laying on of hands of the seven new leaders in the sixth chapter of Acts as support for ordaining deacons. This act apparently followed the Old Testament custom to symbolize the setting apart for divine service and the expressing approval by God's people upon those who would serve (see Num. 8:10).

The ceremony of deacon ordination is a meaningful act of Christian encouragement and recognition. The church members are saying to each person ordained: "We have confidence in you. We will pray for you as you are set apart to minister among us."

Gaines S. Dobbins said: "We do violence to the New Testament and to our Baptist genius when we impute to the ceremony of laying on of hands the conferring of any special qualities or rights. Anything in a Baptist church that an ordained man is authorized to do can be done by an unordained man on authority of the church."[1]

Herschel Hobbs agreed: "Baptists do not hold to the ecclesiastical tradition which leads some to consider ordination the channel through which the ordained receives special ministerial grace or powers not afforded to others. The silence of the New Testament as to the form and meaning of the rite of ordination tends to indicate that it was nothing more than a setting apart or approval of the ordained for the work of ministry."[2]

Churches often devote an entire Sunday worship service to the ordination of deacons. Careful planning can assure that this significant event is a worshipful encounter with God. Early planning allows time for those being ordained to invite relatives, employees and coworkers, and other special friends. The church may send letters or cards of invitation.

Many churches use an examination period just prior to the ordination service. Others incorporate this examination into the ordination service. The intent of this examination is not to screen out those who are unqualified. This will have been done in the earlier screening process. The purpose is more like the questioning and vows in a marriage ceremony. It allows the congregation to hear the deacons publicly share their Christian testimonies, beliefs, and commitments.

Questions can be phrased so deacon nominees can answer simply with "I do" or "I will." It is appropriate to give them guidelines for preparing their testimonies. The candidates will usually include an account of their conversion experience, the subsequent change in their lives, and recent spiritual growth. They may also share their attitude toward the role of deacon and their hopes for the church.

Often two major parts of the ordination service are a charge to the deacons to present the challenge of deacon ministry and a charge to the church to encourage the congregation to support and pray for their deacons. Sometimes these are combined in an ordination sermon.

Acts 6:6 does not clearly say whether the laying on of hands for the new church leaders was done by the entire congregation or only by the apostles. If only ordained pastors and deacons lay on hands, they are doing so as representatives of the congregation. This approach is often taken in larger churches for the sake of time. However, if all church members present lay hands on the deacons, it may heighten the significance of ordination for the whole church and those being ordained. Each person, in laying hands on the deacon's head, usually whispers to the deacon a sentence or two of prayer, an affirmation or challenge, or a verse of

Scripture. An ordination prayer often precedes or follows this part of the service.

The service may also include congregational singing, special music, Scripture reading, prayer, recognition of previously ordained deacons returning to active deacon service, and recognition of the deacons' families. The service usually concludes with the presentation of a Bible or an appropriate book (such as this book) and an ordination certificate to each person being ordained. After the service, the newly ordained deacons and their families can stand at the front of the worship center to be greeted by the congregation. Some churches have a reception following the service.

Preparing Deacons for Effective Ministry

If deacons are to be prepared for effective service, they need training and resources to help them. They will want to learn what their work involves and how they can accomplish it. Since deacons often feel inadequate for areas of ministry in which they have minimal skills, training will have practical value. Deacons who are eager to minister express a desire to be trained for greater effectiveness. A hunger for personal, spiritual growth and for improvement of ministry skills will give deacons a desire for training.

Training can be done in several ways:

- In many churches, deacons are finding that one of the best times for training is the monthly deacons' meeting. They use thirty minutes to an hour of each meeting for training.
- Increasing numbers of churches, associations, and state conventions are sponsoring deacon ministry conferences or retreats to provide this needed training.

- LifeWay Christian Resources provides national deacon ministry conferences and produces materials to train deacons in ministry skills.
- *The Deacon* magazine is a quarterly publication that helps deacons understand their role and assists them in performing their ministries in the church and community.
- This book could be a resource for training.

Unfortunately, some deacons fail to live up to the commitments made at the time of their election and ordination. Deacons who seldom attend worship services, who fail in their responsibilities of ministry, or who dishonor their role disappoint their fellow church members. The congregation should be challenged to relate to them redemptively and forgivingly. Church members should remember Jesus' caution, "The one without sin among you should be the first to throw a stone" (John 8:7). The deacons may have some spiritual, family, financial, or work problems. Some may feel uncomfortable and inadequate in meeting ministry responsibilities because of lack of training. The pastor, deacon officers, and fellow deacons can reach out personally and lovingly to draw them back into fellowship, growth, and service.

Careful screening before election, adequate training, and early sensitivity to warning signals can avoid many dropout problems. Deacons in some churches write their own deacon covenants. These usually state clearly the commitments the deacons are willing to make and how they can help one another live up to those commitments. Guidelines for writing a covenant are suggested by Charles W. Deweese in *The Emerging Role of Deacons*.[3] Deacons can read the covenant responsively or in unison as a part of the annual deacon ordination service.

In summary, the way the church elects, examines, and ordains its deacons should be consistent with what the congregation is seeking—servants for the Lord through his church. Chapters 2 through 5 will focus on who a deacon is. Chapters 6 through 9 will discuss what a deacon does.

CHAPTER 2

Deacons Model
Growth Toward Mature Faith

"I JUST DON'T FEEL QUALIFIED to be a deacon!" This is a common response by potential deacon nominees when approached by the pastor or a screening committee. It is an appropriate response by those who take the biblical qualifications and ministry responsibilities of deacons seriously.

Prospective deacons can appreciate Moses' protest to God, "Who am I, that I should go to Pharaoh and bring the Israelites out of Egypt?" (Exod. 3:11 NIV). When they read the scriptural qualifications of deacons, nominees readily admit their failure to measure up.

The early church had high expectations of both pastors and deacons. The New Testament does not make a great distinction between the qualifications of these partners in pastoral ministry. The basic source of deacon qualifications is found in 1 Timothy 3:8–13. The qualifications of the seven church leaders recorded in Acts 6:3 are also appropriate. These can be grouped into four general qualifications. Those who would be chosen deacons should:

1. Demonstrate growth toward mature faith—"men of good reputation, full of the Spirit and wisdom" (Acts 6:3); "they must keep hold of the deep truths of the faith with a clear conscience" (1 Tim. 3:9 NIV). See chapter 2.

2. Demonstrate Christian family life—"Deacons must be husbands of one wife, managing their children and their own households competently" (1 Tim. 3:12). See chapter 3.

3. Demonstrate personal and public morality—"men of dignity, not double-tongued, or addicted to much wine or fond of sordid gain" (1 Tim. 3:8 NASB). See chapter 4.

4. Demonstrate a life accepted by God and the church—"tested, . . . blameless, . . . those who have served well as deacons acquire a good standing for themselves, and great boldness in the faith" (1 Tim. 3:10, 13). See chapter 5.

The purpose of chapters 2 through 5 is to enable deacons, prospective deacons, and church members voting for deacons to determine who is qualified to serve as a deacon. No one can meet every qualification completely, but deacons should give evidence of progress toward the ideal. The key test is a person's present, continuing behavior. A person's past failure, once discontinued, should be evaluated both in the light of God's promise of renewing forgiveness and in the light of the influence the failure of the past is having on the present. To emphasize the more easily observable qualifications over other factors that are just as important is unwise.

The growing Christian can claim Jesus' promise of life in all its fullness and abundance (John 10:10). The biblical qualifications for deacons suggest that such growth toward mature faith will come in at least four areas—growth in experiencing God's presence (full of the Spirit), in seeing from God's perspective (full of wisdom), in integrating faith into life (holder of the faith), and in demonstrating maturity (good reputation).

Growth in Experiencing God's Presence

Experiencing God's presence has always been central in biblical faith. When God called Abraham to go to a new land, God promised to go with him to show the way (Gen. 12:1). When Moses protested his inadequacy to lead God's people, God responded with the promise, "I will be with you" (Exod. 3:12 NIV). At the Last Supper with his disciples, Jesus was trying to prepare them for the time he would no longer be with them physically. He promised, "I will ask the Father, and He will give you another Counselor to be with you forever. He is the Spirit of truth, . . . the Holy Spirit" (John 14:16–17, 26). When the Jerusalem church needed to set apart new leaders to minister to some special needs and to heal the fellowship, they knew such men needed the fullness of the presence of the Spirit of God (Acts 6:1–6).

Today's deacons need a clear sense of the presence of God's Holy Spirit. Deacons need the strength and power of God's reconciling presence to transform them into persons capable of working with God in ministry to others. Through his indwelling Spirit, God helps deacons grow as persons and to grow in their ability to minister in their church and community. God continues to use deacons who are full of his empowering presence to minister effectively and wondrously among his people (Acts 6:7–8).

Sin creates a barrier to experiencing God's presence. But, rather than spend his time making people feel guilty, Jesus helped them clarify the source of their guilt and the nature of their real problem. The assumption in both the Old Testament and the New Testament is that a person's basic predicament is separation from God. The apostle Paul clearly portrayed this with a variety of parallel words: "ungodly, . . . enemies" (Rom. 5:6, 10), "hostile to God, . . . unable to please God" (Rom. 8:7–8), and "without the Messiah, excluded from the citizenship of Israel, and foreigners to the covenants of the promise, with no hope and without God in the world" (Eph. 2:12). Man's problem is rebellion and thus a lack of relationship with God.

One of the basic results of the sin of rebellion against God is a division within a person himself. Separation from God means a person is not what he can be, what he ought to be.

God does not leave a person in his predicament but gives a promise. God promises salvation to those who recognize their sin as separation from God. The promise is restoration to a right relationship with God. Thus a person can have a relationship with himself that is whole and has meaning and purpose rather than pain and division. He can become his true self and have life in its fullness as God created him to live it.

God's act of reconciliation is through Christ's death on the cross. "We were reconciled to God through the death of His Son" (Rom. 5:10). "But now in Christ Jesus, you who were far away have been brought near by the blood of the Messiah" (Eph. 2:13). In a miraculous and dynamic way, God acted in Christ's death to restore those who accept him to fellowship with God.

Since the barriers are all man-made, God's forgiveness is necessary. Forgiveness means "to send away" or "to wipe away the sin." The past is released and is no longer a barrier that keeps the person from experiencing God's presence. The promise is given that "if we confess our sins, He is faithful and righteous to forgive us our sins and to cleanse us from all unrighteousness" (1 John 1:9).

God can forgive and cancel the sins of the past. In the act of reconciliation through Christ's death, God restores the forgiven sinner to a new relationship.

In addition to the image of reconciliation, Paul and other New Testament writers described this new relationship by turning it as a gem so we could see it in its various dimensions. They speak of the gift of God's peace, which suggests life in harmony with God's will. Another dimension is a new freedom, the deliverance from slavery to sin and the law and the receiving of an inner liberty resulting in service to God and others. Like peace with God and freedom, sonship is a description of what reconciliation means. It is to enter into a unique relationship with God as Father.

Fellowship with God is probably the richest and fullest image of the new relationship a person has with God. This image includes the concepts of communion or koinonia, John's teaching about "abiding in" and "being in" Christ, Paul's doctrine of union with Christ, and other references to seeing and knowing God. What God has done is experienced as a continuing presence of the Spirit of the risen Lord.

Prayer takes on special importance since communication with God is the way to grow in experiencing the intimacy of his loving and gracious presence. Too often the motivation to pray is based on its practical value—"prayer changes things." Such an emphasis is either that prayer is the way God influences or inspires man or that it is the way one informs, influences, or persuades God. However, both of these emphases miss the primary purpose of prayer as conversation with God to build the relationship and to enjoy his presence.

Thus a person should not pray only when "I need it" or "I feel like it." If a husband and wife talk only when they need each other or feel like it, the relationship is in trouble. A growing relationship with a mate or with God needs regular conversation. This usually means a person needs a daily time to focus attention on God's presence.

Activity-oriented, fast-paced living works against a time of prayer. Priorities seem to fill every minute with some kind of activity. The person desiring spiritual growth needs to learn how to make time for God.

Prayer does not bring God's Spirit, but through prayer a person can become aware of God's constant presence. The person who is serious about building his relationship with God through prayer will develop the discipline of silent meditation and listening to God as well as the art of talking to God.

Sometimes the mention of meditation raises the fear of an Eastern form of religious activity that emphasizes detachment from the world. Richard Foster provides a balanced perspective: "Christian meditation goes beyond the notion of detachment. There is a need for detachment, . . . but we must go on to *attachment*. The detachment from the confusion all around us is in order to have a richer attachment to God and to other human beings. Christian meditation leads us to the inner wholeness necessary to give ourselves to God freely."[1]

Jesus demonstrated a necessary balance, a movement back and forth between activity and withdrawal. After describing a day filled with Jesus' teaching and healing, Mark wrote, "Very early in the morning, while it was still dark, He got up, went out, and made His way to a deserted place. And He was praying there" (Mark 1:35). Luke recorded a number of such withdrawals by Jesus for a quiet time of prayer (4:1–13; 5:16; 6:12; 9:28; 11:1; 21:37; 22:39–42).

Many people find devotional materials helpful in guiding a quiet time of devotion and focus on God's presence. Devotional classics provide an opportunity to listen to other people talk of their experiences with God. The greatest devotional classic is the Book of Psalms. The poets' central theme is the fact of God's presence and his involvement in the lives of his people. Reading the Psalms as a part of prayer can help a person learn much about experiencing God's presence in all circumstances of life and expressing praise and thanksgiving for his goodness.

Some people have found it helpful to write down some of their thoughts. God can use this to sort through feelings and focus attention. Written in the awareness of God's presence, this can be a meaningful form of prayer. Occasionally a daily devotional time can be supplemented with a longer period of silence and reflection—a day or two of retreat. Keeping a written record during such an experience is especially beneficial.

A deacon is to be full of the Spirit. The evidence of the deacon's growth in experiencing God's presence is the life he lives. Jesus said: "I am the vine, you are the branches. The one who remains in Me and I in him produces much fruit, because you can do nothing without me. . . . My Father is glorified by this: that you produce much fruit and prove to be My disciples" (John 15:5, 8). Paul wrote that "the fruit of the Spirit is love, joy, peace, patience, kindness, goodness, faith, gentleness, self-control" (Gal. 5:22–23).

Growth in Seeing from God's Perspective

When the Jerusalem church set apart new leaders, they needed men who not only were full of the Spirit but also were full of wisdom. Today's deacons need God's wisdom to carry out their ministry responsibilities.

Surely Jesus would feel the same frustration with his people today that he felt with his disciples. "Do you not yet understand or comprehend? Is your heart hardened? 'Do you have eyes, and not see, and do you have ears, and not hear? And do you not remember?' . . . Don't you understand yet?" (Mark 8:17–18, 21). Christ wants his followers to see as God sees, to see from God's perspective.

God gives wisdom to those who are close to him. God's gift of wisdom includes not only factual knowledge and experience but also the discernment and insight his Spirit can provide. This gift is available to all Christians. "If any of you lacks wisdom, he should ask God, who gives to all generously and without criticizing, and it will be given to him" (James 1:5). James made a distinction between earthly wisdom and wisdom from above (3:13–18). Earthly wisdom, which is motivated by selfish ambition, creates jealousy and disharmony. "But the wisdom from above is first pure, then peace-loving, gentle, compliant, full of mercy and good fruits, without favoritism and hypocrisy" (3:17).

Only repentance and confession of sin enable a person to receive God's forgiveness. Repentance is both an individual's responsibility and God's gift (Acts 3:19, 26). Repentance is not sadness or remorse for sin but a turning away from sin and a return to God in Christ. It involves such a radical reorientation of a person's life that it is called a new birth, resurrection to newness of life, and a new creation.

Conversion is a common term used to describe this life-transforming event. It means "to turn around" or "to change one's belief or view." The same word is used in talking about converting to the metric system of measurement. A real conversion to metrics means a person will think metric and not have to translate from the old terms of measuring. The goal in learning a new language is to think in that language, not just to translate from one's first language. God's goal for his people is that they will think his thoughts and see from his perspective and thus become more like him.

Jesus expressed the reason for seeking God's wisdom, of seeing from God's perspective, in his Model Prayer: "Your kingdom come. Your will be done on earth as it is in heaven" (Matt. 6:10). Paul wrote, "Do not be conformed to this age, but be transformed by the renewing of your mind, so that you may discern what is the good, pleasing, and perfect will of God" (Rom. 12:2).

One of the biggest challenges of seeing from God's perspective is to see oneself as God does. It is much easier to "look at the speck in your brother's eye, but don't notice the log in your own eye" (Luke 6:41). Acknowledging God's truth rather than self-deception is essential for spiritual development. The challenge is that a person neither thinks more highly nor more lowly of himself than God does. Both unconfessed sin and low self-esteem can keep a person from experiencing God's presence.

A person needs to accept responsibility for himself; but fear of weakness may lead to hypocrisy, pretending to be stronger than he is. Difficulty in admitting doubts may lead to outward expressions of false confidence. Disliking wrong decisions, a person may procrastinate. These are expressions of avoiding admission of humanness. God says to this person: "You don't have to hide your true self from me any longer. I know all about you, so you don't have to pretend."

As a person confesses his sin and shares his real self with God and others, he usually finds that his fears were unfounded. He is not reduced by his openness and honesty but is expanded by coming into possession of more of himself. He sees himself as God sees him.

As Elizabeth O'Connor has suggested, not only are we to confess the dark side of life, but we should also confess "our light side. . . . We are responsible and free only as we acknowledge our resources and the fact light has actually penetrated our darkness and made us children of light."[2] As a person confesses this side of himself, he may become aware of abilities, potentialities, and gifts he has repressed along with his faults because they were too threatening to his self-image.

An accurate view of oneself makes it possible to see others as God sees them. A person is more like God when he prefers to forgive the sins of others rather than judge them. If a Christian really understands and receives God's love, forgiveness, patience, kindness, and encouragement, he will want to pass these on to others. Jesus said, "If you forgive people their wrongdoing, your heavenly Father will forgive you as well. But if you don't forgive people, your Father will not forgive your wrongdoing" (Matt. 6:14–15). Apparently God cannot forgive a resentful person. Once Peter asked Jesus, "'Lord, how many times could my brother sin against me and I forgive him? As many as seven times?' 'I tell you, not as many as seven,' Jesus said to him, 'but seventy times seven'" (Matt. 18:21–22). To be effective, deacons must not store up resentments and hurt feelings.

The Christian who sees others as God sees them will not look upon enemies and those who oppose him as objects of contempt and hatred. Instead, he will love his enemies and pray for those who persecute him (Matt. 5:44).

Followers of Jesus will develop his sensitivity and compassion for those who are lost and helpless, like sheep without a shepherd. They will pray with Jesus for more laborers for the harvest (Matt. 9:36–38). They will be motivated to preach the Good News to the lost and provide generous care for those in need. Jesus' followers will see that leadership comes through service and not through status and exercising authority.

Those who see from God's perspective will live in a spirit of joy and thanksgiving based on a confidence in God's steadfast love. Paul encouraged Christians to rejoice in the Lord at all times and to give thanks in all circumstances (1 Thess. 5:16–18). Christians will not be thankful and joyful *for* all circumstances since some bring pain and sadness. But Paul wrote with assurance, "We know that all things work together for the good of those who love God: those who are called according to His purpose" (Rom. 8:28). With wisdom that is beyond human understanding,

Christians can experience God's peace in their hearts and minds (Phil. 4:7).

James warned Christians, "You ask and don't receive because you ask wrongly, so that you may spend it on your desires for pleasure" (James 4:3). Foster stated that "to ask 'rightly' involves transformed passions, total renewal. In prayer, real prayer, we begin to think God's thoughts after him: to desire the things he desires, to love the things he loves. Progressively we are taught to see things from his point of view."[3]

Study of God's Word is the primary way to learn God's perspective. The purpose of such study is not to accumulate information but to be changed into a more Christlike person. In order to truly experience what is read, the Bible student must concentrate and focus attention. Review, repetition, and memorization allow the Spirit to ingrain new thought patterns that transform life. "I have hidden your word in my heart that I might not sin against you" (Ps. 119:11 NIV). Reflecting on the message can bring fresh insight and discernment into life as God intended it to be lived.

Samuel Shoemaker provides a significant warning to deacons who seek God's wisdom and perspective. "The real reason why some of us get such poor guidance, or so little of it, is that we seek direction without being willing to receive conviction first. Unless we let him remove great roadblocks right in front of our doors, we cannot ask him to show us the road."[4]

Deacons who wish to grow toward mature faith will want to grow in seeing from God's perspective. It is toward this goal that Paul prayed for the Ephesian Christians "that He may grant you, according to the riches of His glory, to be strengthened with power through His Spirit in the inner man, and that the Messiah may dwell in your hearts through faith. I pray that you, being rooted and firmly established in love, may be able to comprehend with all the saints what is the breadth and width, height and depth, and to know the Messiah's love that surpasses knowledge, so you may be filled with all the fullness of God" (Eph. 3:16–19).

Growth in Integrating Faith into Life

The goal for deacons is that which the prophets Jeremiah and Ezekiel anticipated—that the Lord would place his law within his people and write it on their hearts (Jer. 31:33; Ezek. 36:27). Deacons who have integrated their faith into their lives are seen as those who hold "the deep truths of the faith with a clear conscience" (1 Tim. 3:9 NIV). They have discovered the joy and freedom that comes from the process of inner growth that expresses itself in outward relationships.

How does God's presence and perspective become real in the deacon's life? How does that which God has done in Christ come to a person where he can feel it as a power that is filling and renewing his life? The Philippian jailer asked, "What must I do to be saved?" Paul and Silas answered, "Believe on the Lord Jesus, and you will be saved" (Acts 16:30–31).

A person responds to God by faith and receives his amazing gift of reconciliation. The New Testament writers used a variety of expressions to speak of this faith response: having faith, believing, confession, repenting, being converted, and becoming as a child.

Faith includes hearing, believing, trusting self to God, and surrender. Paul wrote, "Faith comes from hearing the message" (Rom. 10:17 NIV). Surely a person cannot receive a gift that he does not know about. It is necessary to hear and understand sufficiently about the gift even to respond. Having heard, a person must believe in the basic facts about God's act in Christ. He must believe not only in general but with particularity that God's reconciling act meets him at the point of his own separation from God.

Faith is also trusting one's self to God, not just trusting God in general. It involves giving one's life to God with commitment and without conditions. When a person surrenders to Jesus Christ as Lord, he has made the full turn from the sin of rebellion, the sin of living for himself, to a relationship based on chosen obedience. He chooses obedience as a response to the loving act of God. God has done what an individual is unable to do for himself—reestablish the relationship, to make united what was meant to be united. A person is restored to fellowship with God through the presence of his Holy Spirit.

As a result of the personal response to God's act in Christ, a person not only has his relationship with God renewed but also his relationship with himself. God through Christ enables him to become his true self. When Jesus spoke about the purpose of his life and ministry, he said, "I have come that they may have life and have it in abundance" (John 10:10).

Jesus affirmed that life is to be found in loving relationships. "You shall love the Lord your God with all your heart, with all your soul, with all your strength, and with all your mind; and your neighbor as yourself" (Luke 10:27). If a person sees his life as a gift from God and the heart of that gift as relationships, then the tone of his life will be gratitude to the source and giver of life.

The source of security is found in relationship with God as the source of life. The evidence of this is seen in a trusting dependence on God. Animals and plants demonstrate reliance on divine provision (Luke 12:24–28). The opposite of faith is anxiety and worry. Jesus equated fear with the lack of faith (Mark 4:40). John gave the assurance that whoever abides in God's love will have confidence and not fear (1 John 4:15–18).

Because a person's confidence is based on God's grace and forgiveness, he does not need to obey God's laws in order to be worthy of God's love. Instead God's commands become valuable and appreciated guides for the life that is pleasing to God. "Oh, how I love your law! . . . How sweet are your words to my taste, sweeter than honey to my mouth! I gain understanding from your precepts; therefore I hate every wrong path. Your word is a lamp to my feet and a light for my path" (Ps. 119:97, 103–105 NIV).

The goal is letting God rule in one's life, seeking to know and live obediently according to his will. Jesus declared that this should be the Christian's first priority (Matt. 6:33). His twin parables of the treasure and pearl emphasize that God's will is worth more than everything else a person has (Matt. 13:44–46). When a person is willing to give up everything, that person has reoriented his values according to God's perspective. Jesus made clear how different God's way is from the world's way: "Whoever wants to save his life will lose it, but whoever loses his life because of Me will save it. What is a man benefited if he gains the whole world, yet loses or forfeits himself?" (Luke 9:24–25).

Integrating faith and life means they are combined to achieve unity and harmony. The clear message of Jesus and the New Testament writers is that a genuine experience with God is inseparable from acts of Christlike love.

Growth in Demonstrating Maturity

The seven leaders chosen by the Jerusalem church were men of "good reputation" (Acts 6:3 NASB) or "honest report" (KJV). This means they put into practice the qualities of life discussed in the previous sections.

One of the Seven, Stephen, was brought before the Sanhedrin because he preached boldly. Luke recorded, "All who were sitting in the Sanhedrin looked intently at him and saw that his face was like the face of an angel" (Acts 6:15). Those who are close to God catch and reflect his light. When Moses came down from Mount Sinai with the Ten Commandments, all the people saw how the skin of his face shone because he had been talking with God (Exod. 34:29–30). On the mount of transfiguration, while Jesus "was praying, the appearance of his face changed, and his clothes became dazzling white" (Luke 9:29). Jesus said, "You are the light of the world. . . . Let your light shine before men, so that they may see your good works and give glory to your Father in heaven" (Matt. 5:14, 16).

A little girl told her teacher that she was drawing a picture of God. The teacher said, "But no one knows what God looks like." The little girl replied, "They will when I get through."

Christians may say, "Don't look at me; don't look at the church; look at Jesus." This may not be a statement of humility. It may be said to escape personal responsibility rather than to glorify Jesus. When Philip asked Jesus to show them the Father, Jesus replied: "The one who has seen Me has seen the Father. . . . Don't you believe that I am in the Father and the Father is in Me? The words I speak to you I do not speak on My own. The Father who lives in Me does His works. Believe Me that I am in the Father and the Father is in Me. Otherwise, believe because of the works themselves" (John 14:9–11). Then Jesus told the disciples that because he was going to the Father, God would be giving them the resources of his Spirit. "I assure you: The one who believes in Me will also do the works that I do. And he will do even greater works than these" (John 14:12). This is an amazing promise and challenge.

Becoming a deacon is awesome, but surely it is no less awesome than the challenge Jesus gave to every believer: "Be perfect, therefore, as your heavenly Father is perfect" (Matt. 5:48). This is a reminder that, although deacons serve as examples to the congregation, every Christian is to be measured by the standard of God himself. The Greek word translated "perfect" means "full-grown," "mature," "having reached the appointed end of its development." The Hebrew word means "whole," "entire," "sound."

Paul defined maturity as "the measure of the stature which belongs to the fulness of Christ." He concluded that mature Christians "are no longer to be children" but "are to grow up in all aspects into . . . Christ" (Eph. 4:13–15 NASB). The test by which persons can be sure they are in Christ is to live as Jesus did (1 John 2:5–6). Jesus left an example so believers could follow in his steps (1 Pet. 2:21). "Spiritual transformation is God's work of changing a believer into the likeness of Jesus by creating a new identity in Christ and by empowering a lifelong relationship of love, trust, and obedience to glorify God."[5]

Fred Fisher stated that "the goal of Christian living is likeness to Christ," and then asked if this goal is impossible. He answered both yes and no: "Think of the resources available to the children of God, and it becomes easy to see that it is not impossible to attain such a goal. Men today have the resources available to them that Jesus had available to him. . . . The power of God that enabled him to live the life he lived is available to us also, and on the same terms: absolute commitment of ourselves to God. When we think only of absolute commitment of ourselves to God, we see the task as impossible. Failure lies not in the resources of God; it is man's failure in devotion and surrender to God in Christ."[6]

With such resources available it is not unrealistic to have perfection as a life goal. Gene Wilkes wrote: "Receiving a new spiritual DNA, or a new spiritual code, is an analogy of what happens when you enter a relationship with God through Jesus Christ. God infuses the very code or pattern of God in your spirit. The presence of God's Holy Spirit begins to change you into the likeness of His Son after the pattern of His holiness."[7] A person who has a life commitment to personal growth and maturity is always in process, under construction, becoming the person God created and intended him or her to be.

Many people would like to arrive instantly at the goal of spiritual maturity. As Thomas Merton said, "We do not want to be beginners. But let us be convinced of the fact that we will never be anything else but beginners, all of our life!"[8]

The growing deacon will experience a tension between what he is and what God wants him to become. Such tension is healthy because it pulls the Christian toward the goal of mature faith. Paul admitted that he had not arrived at the goal of perfection, but he was determined to "press on toward the goal for the prize of the upward call of God in Christ Jesus" (Phil. 3:14 NASB). He added that those who are perfect or mature would have that attitude—a drive toward the continuing change and growth needed to conform to the image of Christ.

Growth into Christlikeness is a gift from God, but Christians must discipline themselves in order to be open to receive this gift. The inner transformation that will express itself in outward relationships is worth the effort.

When I was a teenager, I had a motto on my wall, "Anything worth doing is worth doing well." This was a challenge to excellence. A friend rephrased the motto, "Anything worth doing is worth doing badly." He was saying that doing anything well requires going through the painful process of failure. Falling down is a part of learning to walk or to ride a bicycle. T. B. Maston emphasized this dimension of Christian growth: "God's creative men and women are those who are stirred from within by a dream that causes them to attempt more than they can do or be. They are never satisfied, but they are not frustrated or defeated. They believe that the One who gives the dream is understanding of the dreamer and forgives him of his failures."[9]

How rewarding for deacons, as Christian leaders, to be able to say with Paul, "Join in following my example" (Phil. 3:17 NASB). This word comes immediately after Paul admitted he had not arrived at perfection and was committed to a life of growth. That is what others need—a look at someone whose life is in the process of becoming more Christlike. The Christian life becomes an exciting possibility for all.

Deacons who are demonstrating growth in experiencing God's presence, in seeing from God's perspective, and in integrating faith into life have a unique opportunity to model mature faith in the church.

CHAPTER 3

Deacons Model Christian Family Life

THE DEACON'S FAMILY FACES some unique expectations because church members have developed a high view of the deacon role. Of course, both realistic and unrealistic expectations are a part of this view.

The deacon's family should not be expected to be perfect, but family members do have the opportunity to model Christian family life. Such modeling should be primarily in response to their relationship to Christ and not just to live up to the deacon role.

Paul indicated what churches in the first century expected of their deacons. A deacon was to be the husband of one wife and to manage his children and family well. The deacon's wife was expected to demonstrate the same high standards as her husband (1 Tim. 3:11–12). These biblical qualifications suggest four areas that deacons, potential deacons, and church members voting for deacons can use to determine who is qualified to serve as a deacon. These four areas are the deacon's marriage, the deacon's wife, the deacon's parent-child relationship, and the deacon's family life.

The Deacon's Marriage

Both pastors and deacons were to have only one wife (1 Tim. 3:2,12). Certainly, in his cultural setting Paul meant men who were practicing polygamy, those married to more than one wife at a time, were unacceptable for these church leadership positions. However, Paul's primary emphasis was that a deacon must be a "one-woman man."

Usually churches interpret this qualification to disqualify those who have been divorced and have remarried. Most of these churches also disqualify those who are divorced but have never remarried. This view is held because Jesus strongly emphasized the sanctity of marriage (Mark 10:2–12). Other churches agree that the ideal is no divorce and no remarriage. However, these churches say a person who has divorced can receive God's renewing forgiveness and thus is eligible for election as a deacon in the same way as another person who has been forgiven for violations of other qualifications. When a church is determining its policy on the eligibility of divorced persons, it is best for the members to discuss and adopt the guidelines when no specific personalities are involved.

Some churches interpret "the husband of one wife" to mean all deacons should be married rather than single. However, this would seem to contradict Paul's encouragement to the unmarried to remain single because he thought the end of time was near (1 Cor. 7:8, 25–28, 32). In the same passage Paul apparently approved but did not encourage remarriage after the death of a spouse (1 Cor. 7:8–9, 39). Thus, those who are single could be eligible for deacon service.

In considering this qualification concerning marriage, churches should not limit their attention to the issue of divorce. Certainly Paul was primarily concerned about the faithfulness by the husband and wife to their marriage relationship. In their marriage ceremony a husband and wife made a "for better or worse" commitment to each other. This was a promise to work at developing the relationship and overcoming barriers.

When God created woman as a helper and companion to man, his purpose was that "a man shall leave his father and his mother, and shall cleave to his wife; and they shall become one flesh" (Gen. 2:24 NASB). When Jesus quoted this verse, he concluded, "What God has joined together, man must not separate" (Matt. 19:6). Sexual fidelity is only one part of this union. The husband and wife should also refuse to let a job, their children, leisure activities, parents, community responsibilities, or even the church come between them.

In his letter to the church at Ephesus, Paul declared a basic principle of relationships. Christians are to relate to other Christians in mutual submission based on their reverence for Christ (Eph. 5:21). He then discussed the marriage relationship (Eph. 5:22–33). He pointed to Christ's relationship to the church as a guide for husbands and wives relating to each other.

In Paul's day the wife was already supposed to be submissive to her husband. The unique emphasis by Paul was giving decision-making status to women who had no legal standing in that culture. A Christian wife could freely choose to submit to her husband in the same way she had freely chosen to submit to the Lord.

The primary burden of change was on the husband. His example was Christ's relationship as head of the church, but that role is expressed not through control but through love. Such love requires sacrifice by the husband for the good of his wife. As Christ did not come to be served but to serve, the husband is to care for his wife. His love for his wife has the same purpose as his love for himself—to enable growth in becoming the holy and pure person God desires. As in any close relationship, differences will lead to occasional conflicts; but the Christian husband and wife will seek God's guidance to resolve the conflict for the good of both.

The marriage relationship provides an excellent opportunity for the deacon to be a servant model in the church. This is especially true since marriage is often used in the Old Testament as an illustration of the relationship of God and his people and in the New Testament of Christ's relationship with his church.

The Deacon's Wife

In the section on qualifications for deacons, Paul inserted some qualifications for the "women" (1 Tim. 3:11 HCSB, NASB) or the "wives" (KJV, NIV). Interpreters have disagreed on whether this refers to wives of deacons, deaconesses or women deacons, wives of both pastors (overseers) and deacons, or women in general. The last two have little support. In the New Testament the Greek word is sometimes clearly used to mean "wife" (see 1 Cor. 7:2; Eph. 5:22; 1 Pet. 3:1). At other times it is clearly used to mean "woman" (see Mark 5:25; Luke 15:8; Acts 5:14).

The evidence in the 1 Timothy 3 passage clearly applies to deacons' wives. If Paul had intended to refer to women deacons, he probably would have used a more specific term since he used the same word in the next verse to indicate wife. The discussion flows more naturally if it applies to deacons (vv. 8–10), deacons' wives (v. 11), and deacons' married and family life (v. 12).

A few churches do elect women as deacons. If they do so, they do not primarily support their action by this passage. Their emphasis is on Christ's relating to women as persons at a time when they were considered little more than property. Paul emphasized a new equality in Christ. "There is no Jew or Greek, slave or free, male or female; for you are all one in Christ Jesus" (Gal. 3:28). They also point out that women are often portrayed in the New Testament in the caring role of servants consistent with the ministry tasks of deacons. Women had roles of leadership in the early church (see Acts 18:26; 21:9; 1 Cor. 11:5). Women also have responsibilities as leaders in today's churches. These churches feel that Paul's assumption that deacons were men was because of the male-dominated cultural setting and is not binding in a culture where women have greater freedom and responsibility. At various times in church history some churches have elected women to serve as deacons.[1]

However, most churches have decided to elect only men as deacons and encourage wives to serve in a team ministry with their husbands. These churches acknowledge that God uses women as well as men to minister to the needs of people in the church and community, but they feel that the deacon role should be reserved for men. A church will decide whether to elect women as deacons based on its understanding of biblical teaching, its understanding of the role of women and the marriage relationship, and its commitment to maintaining a positive fellowship in the church.

Certainly Paul's primary emphasis is on qualifications. He wrote that the deacons' wives "must likewise be dignified, not malicious gossips, but temperate, faithful in all things" (1 Tim. 3:11 NASB). When Paul used the word *likewise* both here and in verse 8, he seemed to say that readers should not focus on the differences in the lists of qualifications for pastors, deacons, and wives. The early church had high expectations for all its leaders.

Deacons' wives are expected to be "dignified" (NASB). They are to conduct themselves in ways that make them "worthy of respect" (HCSB, NIV). The Greek word comes from a root word that means "godly," "devout," or "reverent." This implies that they honor and serve God as a natural manner of life. This is the same word used to describe deacons in verse 8. This characteristic means both deacons and wives will have the respect and confidence of their church and community.

Wives are also not to be malicious gossips. Deacons are not to be "double-tongued" and wives are not to be devil-tongued. The English word *diabolical* comes from the word translated here as "slanderers" (HCSB, KJV) or "gossips" (NASB). Often the word is translated "devil" (Matt. 4:1) or "false accuser" (2 Tim. 3:3 KJV). Deacons and their wives must be servants who build people up and not be slanderers who spread false charges that damage reputations.

The wives of deacons are also to be "temperate" (1 Tim. 3:11 NASB, NIV). Through the strength of God's presence, they are "self-controlled" (HCSB). They are "sober" (KJV) in the sense of being free of physical, mental, emotional, and spiritual excesses. Instead of being confused and rash in their decisions, they exercise self-restraint. This quality contributes to stability in the home and in the church.

Faithfulness is another quality needed in deacons' wives. People in the church and community will look to them for an example and in times of need. They are known for being reliable and trustworthy. This includes loyalty to God, home, church, and other people.

The Deacon's Parent-Child Relationship

Deacons are to manage their children well (1 Tim. 3:12). Many deacons and potential deacons feel especially unqualified at this point. A toddler's fussiness, a child's persistent talking, a teenager's mood swings can often bring out the worst in parents. Being a parent is a humbling experience. Deacons will not be perfect parents, but church members facing the same struggle to be effective Christian parents will look to their deacons to see how they relate to their children.

In the passage on mutual submission by Christians, Paul also discussed the relationship between parents and children (Eph. 6:1–4). The application of the sixth commandment to honor parents was that children should obey them. Paul's unique emphasis was that Christian children would choose to obey their parents because of their relationship with the Lord. In a parallel passage Paul wrote, "Children, obey your parents in everything, for this is pleasing in the Lord" (Col. 3:20).

During a child's developing years the primary burden of responsibility is on the Christian parent. "Fathers, don't stir up anger in your children, but bring them up in the training and instruction of the Lord" (Eph. 6:4). In the previous chapter Paul used the word translated "bring up" to describe how a person cares for his own body and how Christ cares for the church (Eph. 5:29).

Parental discipline involves setting limits for the child and seeing that the child learns to live within those boundaries. This will include direction, teaching, and sometimes enforcement through appropriate punishment. The purpose of the discipline is to help the child mature into a person who can and will discipline himself.

Many parents have told their children, "If I didn't love you, I wouldn't care what you did." The writer of Hebrews reminded his readers of the proverb, "The Lord disciplines whom He loves" (Heb. 12:6; from Prov. 3:12). Speaking of discipline both by the Lord and by a parent, he concluded, "No discipline seems enjoyable at the time, but painful. Later on, however, it yields the fruit of peace and righteousness to those who have been trained by it" (Heb. 12:11).

A child being punished may find it hard to believe a parent who says, "This hurts me as much as it hurts you." But seeking to provide the guidance a child needs is a painful process for parents. Parents want to "train a child in the way he should go" so that "when he is old he will not turn from it" (Prov. 22:6 NIV). They try to avoid being either too lenient or too strict. Sometimes parents feel it difficult to separate necessary firmness and their own anger. They need to seek an appropriate balance between allowing and limiting freedom.

Not only are Christian parents to provide discipline, but they are also to give "instruction of the Lord" (Eph. 6:4). This includes warning, correcting, admonishing, and reminding of what is right and wrong in God's sight.

After proclaiming God's law to the people of Israel, Moses added this word from the Lord: "These words, which I am commanding you today, shall be on your heart; and you shall teach them diligently to your sons and shall talk of them when you sit in your house and when you walk by the way and when you lie down and when you rise up" (Deut. 6:6–7 NASB). Parents have the responsibility for a child's growth. They cannot turn their child's moral and spiritual development over to the school and church.

Parents will seek to provide the kind of guidance and home environment in which a child can learn God's way. Instruction will be both in words and in example. A teenage boy expressed appreciation to his parents: "I'm glad I have Christian parents who don't just tell me how to live, but I can see they do it too." Deacons can first of all be servant models in their own home.

Paul cautioned parents that some forms of discipline and instruction may provoke children to anger. If a child feels his parents' expectations are impossible to meet, discouragement is the inevitable result. Continuous criticism can break a child's spirit. Setting rules, saying no, punishing, and correcting are all a part of discipline; but these negative forms should be more than balanced with positive expressions of encouragement. Children need parents who will listen attentively, answer their questions, play with them, and show them affection.

Often the question is asked, "How do children spell love?" The answer is that children spell love "TIME." When parents give time to their children, they have given themselves. That is the only unique gift a parent can offer.

The Deacon's Family Life

Deacons are also to manage their families well (1 Tim. 3:12). The deacon's family can demonstrate Christian family life through relationships, priorities in decision making, and by handling crises and problems redemptively.

One of the challenges of family life is to find the right balance between the husband-wife relationship and the parent-child relationship. Some people give so much of their energy and time to their children that they neglect their marriage. When children observe a strong and growing bond between their father and mother, they have a greater sense of security. The parents can demonstrate healthy interdependence and mutual submission in love.

What Paul said about the members of the church as the body of Christ could be said about family members. "If one member suffers, all the members suffer with it; if one member is honored, all the members rejoice with it" (1 Cor. 12:26). In a Christian home when family members acknowledge their hurts, failures, and imperfection, they should receive comfort, forgiveness, and encouragement. Often this can be done in the setting of family worship. The success or recognition of one family member can become an occasion for the whole family to celebrate and express thanks to God.

A necessary part of managing a family well is developing some structure for smooth functioning. This may include dividing up the chores, determining a daily schedule, developing family rituals, and respecting others' rights.

A sign of effective family life is the increasing maturity of the children. The family has provided a healthy environment that has encouraged growth in decision making, accepting responsibility, and self-discipline. Thus a child who reaches adulthood is prepared to leave father and mother to establish a separate home.

Many deacons find that other people enjoy being in their home because "your family is different." That difference is the quality of Christian relationships. The deacon's family can help other families see that an appropriate balance of meaningful family life, caring ministry, and active church involvement can be achieved.

CHAPTER 4

Deacons Model
Personal and Public Morality

DEACONS SHOULD BE PERSONS of exemplary Christian character in their personal and public lives. Paul wrote that the first-century churches expected their deacons to be persons who are "grave, not doubletongued, not given to much wine, not greedy of filthy lucre" (1 Tim. 3:8 KJV).

These biblical expectations suggest four qualifications to identify those who would be deacons. Deacons should have respected conduct, a controlled tongue, a Spirit-controlled body, and right priorities.

Respected Conduct

Sometimes the Greek word translated "grave" (KJV) is translated "worthy of respect" (HCSB) or "dignity" (NASB). Deacons are to be serious and dignified. In Paul's letter to Titus he wrote, "Set an example of good works yourself, with integrity and dignity in your teaching. Your message is to be sound beyond reproach, so that the opponent will be ashamed, having nothing bad to say about us" (Titus 2:7–8).

This means deacons will conduct themselves in a manner that will make them worthy of the respect of others. Peter challenged his readers, "Conduct yourselves honorably among the Gentiles, so that in a case where they speak against you as those who do evil, they may, by observing your good works, glorify God" (1 Pet. 2:12).

41

This Greek word comes from a root word that is sometimes translated "piety" or "godliness." Paul encouraged Timothy to train himself in godliness. Although training the body is important, Paul emphasized that spiritual fitness has greater benefit. Godliness is necessary both for the present life and for the life to come (1 Tim. 4:7–8). Cornelius the centurion was described as a godly or devout man. He worshiped God, gave generously to help others, and was consistent in prayer (Acts 10:2).

A pastor remembered two deacons who took their role seriously. "Each was cooperative, accessible to those in need, compassionate, faithful in all respects to the Lord and to the church. While both were limited in educational background, this did not hinder their image as men who walked circumspectly and provided a Christian witness during their everyday lives." The pastor wrote that the first of these deacons "was respected in the community. . . . He had gained the reputation of being a fair and honest man. When he spoke, people listened; for they knew he had something to say. . . . [He] lived his Christianity. He lived it in his thoughts but also in his words and in his actions." Of the other deacon, the pastor wrote: "His prayers were common; yet they voiced his concern, compassion, and love in such a way that there could be no doubt that these prayers came from the heart of a godly man. His enthusiasm was infectious, encouraging the congregation to do more for their Lord than they had ever done before."[1]

Jesus harshly criticized those who gave alms, prayed, and fasted in ways to attract the acclaim of others (Matt. 6:1–2, 5, 16); but he also said his followers are the light of the world and should not be hidden. He commanded, "Let your light shine before men, so that they may see your good works and give glory to your Father in heaven" (Matt. 5:16).

A test of a deacon's true character is his attitude toward having his life revealed by the light. If his actions are ungodly, he will avoid being seen by others; but if he is godly, he does not seek attention but is willing to let his deeds be seen and to give God the credit (John 3:19–21).

Deacons whose conduct is respected by others will naturally be selected to serve in roles of leadership both in their churches and in their communities. They should be encouraged to accept such responsibilities. Their dignified and godly service that glorifies God will be a source of strength and stability not only to the churches but also to the communities.

A Controlled Tongue

Deacons are not to be "double-tongued" (1 Tim. 3:8 NASB). This word literally means "double-worded." Deacons must be consistent in their speech if others are to consider them persons of integrity rather than duplicity. *Merriam-Webster's Collegiate Dictionary* defines *duplicity* as "contradictory doubleness of thought, speech, or action."

A church does not expect deacons to be eloquent speakers, but church members do want them to speak with clarity rather than confusion. Paul warned, "If the trumpet makes an unclear sound, who will prepare for battle? In the same way, unless you use your tongue for intelligible speech, how will what is spoken be known?" (1 Cor. 14:8–9). Paul told Timothy that persons in the church who fight over words only undermine the faith of others. Instead God approves of those who can accurately proclaim God's Word (2 Tim. 2:14–15).

Moses protested to the Lord: "Please, Lord, I have never been eloquent . . . for I am slow of speech and slow of tongue." God answered: "Who has made man's mouth? . . .

Is it not I, the Lord? Now then go, and I, even I, will be with your mouth, and teach you what you are to say" (Exod. 4:10–12 NASB). When deacons are sensitive to God's guiding presence, they can communicate clearly and adequately.

James seems to have the idea of double-tongued or double-worded in mind when he said that the tongue can be used "to give thanks to our Lord and Father and also to curse our fellow-man, who is created in the likeness of God. Words of thanksgiving and cursing pour out from the same mouth. My brothers, this should not happen! No spring of water pours out sweet water and bitter water from the same opening" (James 3:9–11 GNB).

Jesus expanded the commandment prohibiting murder to include words of contempt for another human being. He then declared that such a person should take the initiative to be reconciled to his brother before his worship of God would be acceptable (Matt. 5:21–24). Both James and John stated that persons cannot claim to have faith in God and to have received his love if their words of mercy are not backed up with acts of mercy (James 2:14–17; 1 John 3:17–18).

The ninth commandment prohibits false witness. A witness convicted of accusing another falsely was to receive the punishment intended for the accused (Deut. 19:16–19). One of the Greek words most often translated "devil" is sometimes translated "false accuser," "malicious gossip," or "slanderer." It is the word used in the qualifications of deacons' wives (1 Tim. 3:11). Certainly a person who damages another's reputation could be called a devil. The deacon's goal is to build people up, and thus he could be called Barnabas, a son of encouragement (Acts 4:36).

People who pretend to be good but who are dishonest and deceitful are also double-tongued. Jesus condemned the scribes and Pharisees for such hypocrisy. He accused them of carefully tithing but neglecting justice, mercy, and faithfulness. They looked clean on the outside but inside were full of robbery and self-indulgence. They were like tombs whitewashed to look nice, but they contained dead men's bones and rottenness. They looked like good men but were really full of pretense and crime (Matt. 23:23–28). Being double-tongued includes saying one thing to one group and another thing to another group. Such hypocrisy is too often the source of church conflict.

Churches need deacons who are true to their word and can be trusted. A person who cheats on his income tax or pads his expense account betrays such trust. Unfortunately, some people are dishonest with the government or with a company who would never think of being dishonest to another person. Sometimes being honest and sticking to one's promise will require sacrifice (Ps. 15:4). Some deacons have chosen to change jobs rather than to participate in their employer's unethical practices.

Deacons must also commit themselves to confidentiality. They will be entrusted with the knowledge of the personal lives of church members. They should repeat confidential information only when they have permission.

James wrote that the person who is able to control what he says is able to control his whole body. He also said no one can tame the tongue, implying that such control only comes with God's indwelling presence. The controlled tongue is compared to the bit in a horse's mouth or the rudder on a ship. Under the control of a skilled rider or pilot, the horse will obey and the ship will remain on course (James 3:2–8).

Deacons who have controlled tongues know when to speak and when to remain silent and listen. They will sense when it is appropriate to comfort and when it is appropriate to confront. They will seek always to speak the right word at the right time in a spirit of love.

A Spirit-Controlled Body

Paul indicated that first-century deacons were not to be "given to much wine" (1 Tim. 3:8 KJV). Most Baptist churches require their deacons to abstain totally from any alcoholic beverages. Many people wish Paul had omitted "much," so this qualification would clearly support total abstinence. However, since water was relatively scarce and often polluted in biblical times, wine was used as a basic drink in everyday meals. The wine was usually fermented grape juice.

The word *given* is sometimes translated "addicted." Such translations may give the impression that moderate social drinking is acceptable as long as it does not lead to drunkenness or addiction. But if Paul had meant that deacons should not get drunk, he could have used the word he used other times which clearly means "intoxication" and "drunkenness" (see Rom. 13:13; Gal. 5:21). If he had meant addiction, he could have used the word meaning "enslaved" (Titus 2:3).

The word *given* means "to pay attention to" or "be concerned about." Only a few verses before, Paul applied a different Greek word that means "being near, beside, or in the vicinity of wine" (1 Tim. 3:3). Apparently Paul was intending to place severe limits on the use of wine by pastors (overseers) and deacons. The imagery of Paul's words is similar to the psalmist's commendation of those who do not even associate with evil. "Blessed is the man who does not walk in the counsel of the wicked, nor stand in the path of sinners, nor sit in the seat of scoffers" (Ps. 1:1 NASB).

The biblical writers sometimes praise wine but more often they strongly condemn it. Wine often appears in parallel to "strong drink," which refers to more intensely alcoholic intoxicants in general. The familiar proverb stated,

"Wine is a mocker, strong drink a brawler, and whoever is intoxicated by it is not wise" (Prov. 20:1 NASB). Isaiah warned of spiritual blindness by those who daily use wine and strong drink. "They do not pay attention to the deeds of the Lord, nor do they consider the work of His hands" (Isa. 5:12 NASB). Paul included drunkenness in his list of deeds of the flesh that he contrasted with the fruit of the Spirit (Gal. 5:19–23). He suggested that Christians should avoid immoral people, idolaters, and drunkards if they claim to be brothers since their lives contradict that claim (1 Cor. 5:11).

Paul also raised the issue that responsibility for others is more important than personal freedom. "It is a noble thing not to eat meat, or drink wine, or do anything that makes your brother stumble" (Rom. 14:21). Wine and strong drink do enslave and destroy bodies. However, concern for weaker brothers alone should be sufficient reason for a thoughtful deacon to abstain totally from any alcoholic beverages.

The tragic effects of wine on the body and mind are graphically described in Proverbs 23:29–35 (NASB):

Who has woe? Who has sorrow? Who has contentions? Who has complaining? Who has wounds without cause? Who has redness of eyes? Those who linger long over wine, those who go to taste mixed wine. Do not look on the wine when it is red, when it sparkles in the cup, when it goes down smoothly; at the last it bites like a serpent, and stings like a viper. Your eyes will see strange things, and your mind will utter perverse things. And you will be like one who lies down in the middle of the sea, or like one who lies down on the top of a mast. "They struck me, but I did not become ill; they beat me, but I did not know it. When shall I awake? I will seek another drink."

The Christian's body is the temple of the Holy Spirit (1 Cor. 6:19). The Christian must not dissipate that body or desecrate that temple by getting drunk with wine. Rather, he must be filled with God's presence and thus be controlled by the Spirit (Eph. 5:18). In contrast to the results of wine described in Proverbs, Paul wrote that control by God's Spirit finds expression in worshiping him with praise and thanksgiving and in mutually submissive relationships (Eph. 5:19–6:9).

Paul encouraged care for the physical body. For health reasons he suggested to Timothy, "Don't continue drinking only water, but use a little wine because of your stomach and your frequent illnesses" (1 Tim. 5:23). Apparently Timothy had chosen to abstain totally from wine. Paul reminded him that the medicinal use of wine was sometimes appropriate, but this counsel cannot be used to justify the use of wine or other alcoholic beverages in the twenty-first century.

A present-day parallel might be the use of prescription drugs. Paul would certainly see their health value and encourage their appropriate use for that purpose. However, he would probably caution against excessive use that leads to dependence and thus control by the drugs rather than the Holy Spirit. Paul might also suggest that deacons avoid any other excesses that pollute or control their bodies. Today's churches need deacons who have Spirit-controlled bodies.

Right Priorities

Deacons are not to be "greedy of filthy lucre" (1 Tim. 3:8 KJV). Actually the word *greedy* is not used in the Greek. Apparently, Paul intended the word *given* from the previous phrase to apply here too. Again it means "to pay attention to" or "be concerned about." That includes greed but is much broader.

In the qualifications for pastors (overseers), Paul used a different word meaning "free from the love of money" (1 Tim. 3:3 NASB). Paul warned Timothy, "The love of money is a root of all kinds of evil" (1 Tim. 6:10). Such a craving can lead persons to wander away from their faith in God.

Paul's primary concern is that deacons have right priorities. Their attitude toward money is a good measure of those priorities. Jesus said, "You cannot be slaves of God and of money" (Matt. 6:24). Many people are so committed to what money can get—pleasure, status, power—that it enslaves them. Jesus urged: "Don't worry about your life, what you will eat or what you will drink; or about your body, what you will wear. Isn't life more than food and the body more than clothing? . . . The Gentiles eagerly seek all these things, and your heavenly Father knows that you need them. But seek first the kingdom of God and His righteousness, and all these things will be provided for you" (Matt. 6:25, 32–33).

Deacons who trust God rather than money as their source of security can be free from the temptation to worship their possessions. They find new meaning in the prayer, "Give us today our daily bread" (Matt. 6:11). They realize that God intends for everyone to have adequate food, clothing, and shelter.

The tenth commandment prohibits covetousness. James declared that obsession for possessions distorts a person's relationships with others and with God. "You desire and do not have. You murder and covet and cannot obtain. You fight and war. . . . You ask and don't receive because you ask wrongly, so that you may spend it on your desires for pleasure" (James 4:2–3).

Paul demonstrated that a person does not need to despise or live for possessions. He wrote the Philippian church: "I have learned to be content in whatever circumstances I am. I know both how to have a little, and I know how to have a lot. In any and all circumstances I have learned the secret of being content—whether well-fed or hungry, whether in abundance or in need. I am able to do all things through Him who strengthens me" (Phil. 4:11–13).

The only person Jesus asked to sell all he had in order to follow him was the rich young ruler. Though a moral person, Jesus saw that he was addicted to his possessions. He needed to release them in order to place his trust in Jesus. People who are "given to filthy lucre" are money abusers. Greed is an addiction to money and possessions.

The word translated "filthy lucre" means "shameful monetary gain," "dishonest profit," or "dishonorable advantage." Paul does not reject the value of an employee making an honest living or an employer making a fair profit. He does cause deacons to ask serious economic questions in the light of biblical principles of personal and public morality.

Deacons need to ask if their work is honest and honors God. They must also examine their motives. Are they primarily concerned only about self and family and thus willing to ignore or even take advantage of others? The prophets pronounced the Lord's harsh judgment on such people. "Your eyes and your heart are intent only upon your own dishonest gain, and on shedding innocent blood and on practicing oppression and extortion" (Jer. 22:17 NASB).

However, biblical writers commend those who use their possessions, whether great or small, to help others. Barnabas and others in the early church sold property to help the needy in the congregation (Acts 4:32–37). James and John declared that those who use their resources to help the hungry and the needy are demonstrating that they have faith and possess God's love (James 2:14–17; 1 John 3:17–18). Jesus told the parable of the good Samaritan who generously helped a stranger in need and even accepted continuing financial responsibility for him (Luke 10:30–37).

Most churches expect their deacons to give at least a tithe of their income. Tithing is one way Christians acknowledge that all income and possessions are gifts from God. Many deacons have discovered the joy of freely giving beyond the tithe for missions and other church needs. They use their time and resources quietly and generously to minister to persons. Some volunteer their special skills in their church, community, or on a mission field.

Deacons who have right priorities will be released from anxiety, selfishness, and greed. More than anything else, they will desire God's kingdom, his rule in their lives.

Paul told Timothy, "Be an example to the believers in speech, in conduct, in love, in faith, in purity" (1 Tim. 4:12). Deacons not only represent the kingdom of God in general; they also represent their local church in the community. Deacons have the challenge and the opportunity to model personal and public morality through respected conduct, a controlled tongue, a Spirit-controlled body, and right priorities. The need for these characteristics to describe the life of a deacon cannot be overemphasized.

CHAPTER 5

Deacons Model a Life Accepted by God and the Church

CHURCH MEMBERS WHO VOTE to elect deacons for the church carry a burden of responsibility. Paul wrote that potential deacons should "be tested first; if they prove blameless, then they can serve as deacons" (1 Tim. 3:10).

The election of deacons is not a popularity contest. Rather, the church should elect only those who have given evidence that they are qualified for this important role. This is the primary reason most churches require persons to be members for a period of time before they are eligible to be elected as deacons. This gives church members an opportunity to observe a person's growth toward mature faith, Christian family life, personal and public morality, and ministry as partners.

Such testing or proving is important because the qualities expected of deacons are expected of all Christians. Deacons demonstrating those qualities as deacons will be examples to the rest of the congregation.

Jesus and the New Testament writers warned that not everyone in the church is adequately living the Christian life. Jesus said, "Beware of false prophets who come to you in sheep's clothing, but inwardly are ravaging wolves. You'll recognize them by their fruit. Are grapes gathered from thornbushes or figs from thistles? In the same way, every good tree produces good fruit, but a bad tree produces bad fruit. . . . Not everyone who says to Me, 'Lord, Lord!' will enter the kingdom of heaven, but the one who does the will of My Father in heaven" (Matt. 7:15–17, 21). Church members must inspect the fruit of a potential deacon (and a potential deacon must examine himself) to see if he is living a life that is acceptable to both God and the church.

Accepted by God

Salvation is a gift from God that recipients cannot earn. They can only receive God's gift in grateful faith and surrender. That response includes a commitment to know and obey God's will.

The word translated "tested" comes from a root word meaning "watch." The Christian lives under the watchful eye of God. The psalmist understood and knew the value of God's examination and judgment. "O Lord, you have searched me and you know me. . . . Search me, O God, and know my heart; test me and know my anxious thoughts. See if there is any offensive way in me, and lead me in the way everlasting" (Ps. 139:1, 23–24 NIV).

Those who live in the light are not afraid to have God see their thoughts and actions. Their goal and ambition is to learn and do what pleases him (Eph. 5:10; 2 Cor. 5:9). Pleasing God is the way to express gratitude for his gift of forgiveness and new life. Thus the acceptable act of sacrificial worship is to offer a holy life to God (Rom. 12:1). When the pressure to conform to the world is resisted and transformation is accomplished by the Spirit of God, a Christian can have a clear understanding of God's will. His will is that which is good for the person, is acceptable to God, and is perfect as God is perfect (Rom. 12:2; Matt. 5:48).

Jesus gave himself as the example of pleasing God through obedience to him and dependence on his presence (John 8:28–29). Churches will look for its prospective deacons among church members who are following Christ's example and thus are acceptable and pleasing to God.

Accepted by the Church

Church members have the responsibility to determine who is accepted by God and thus acceptable to the church. In one of his parables, Jesus told of a man who purchased five yoke of oxen and needed to try them out (Luke 14:19). He needed to test them like a person today would road test a car he was considering buying. Churches will examine the Christian character and the ministry record of each person being considered for the role of deacon.

Church members cannot search the heart or thoughts of a person. They can evaluate only on the basis of words, attitudes, and actions. They will assume that the fruit they can see is evidence of a personal relationship with Christ.

One of the most obvious ways church members will test potential deacons is attendance at church activities. At first this may appear to be a superficial approach. Although an attendance record will not become the only test of commitment, regular participation in church ministries can reveal much about a person.

People who are faithful to the Sunday worship services communicate a desire to praise and thank God, to celebrate life with Christian friends, and to be comforted and confronted by God's Word. By consistent Bible study attendance, people indicate an awareness of their continuing need to learn more about God, their relationship with him, and his way for their lives. Active participation in discipleship lifts up the value of being equipped as a more effective Christian and church member. Attendance at the midweek service reveals a commitment to prayer for persons in the church family and a need for spiritual refreshment.

Most churches expect their deacons to make a spoken commitment to give at least a tithe of their income. Other churches expect deacons to be committed to growing in financial stewardship. Of course, church members will not know how much money others give to the church. They will be impressed primarily by the attitudes potential deacons have toward money in general and by their commitment to the ministries and mission efforts that church offerings support. Paul commended the Macedonian churches for their generosity in giving even beyond their limited means to provide aid to the poor Christians in Jerusalem (2 Cor. 8:14). He urged the Corinthians to share in such generous offerings and thus "prove the sincerity of your love" (2 Cor. 8:8 KJV).

Church members will also evaluate the doctrinal soundness of potential deacons. John cautioned, "Do not believe every spirit, but test the spirits to determine if they are from God, because many false prophets have gone out into the world" (1 John 4:1). John applied this to such key doctrines as the incarnation (1 John 4:2), the necessity of admitting and confessing sins (1 John 1:8–10), and the Christian's release from sin's control (1 John 3:4–10). God approves those who clearly believe, speak, and live his word of truth (2 Tim. 2:15).

Since deacons are servant models in the church, church members will seek to elect those who are already ministering to the needs of people. They will observe the support and ministry given by potential deacons to the pastor and other church leaders. They will also notice kindness and practical care for the least of Christ's brothers in the church and community.

Potential deacons must be found blameless not only in church participation, sound doctrine, and ministry to persons, but also in Christian character. Their lives should be exemplary so no charge such as immorality or dishonesty can be brought against them. Deacons should not be involved in activities that would weaken their witness or embarrass the church. In his list of the works of the flesh, Paul included hatred, quarreling, jealousy, bad temper, self-ishness, dissension, factions, and envy as well as sexual immorality, idolatry, and drunkenness (Gal. 5:19–21). Those who are blameless will demonstrate the fruit of the Spirit: "love, joy, peace, patience, kindness, goodness, faith, gentleness, self-control" (Gal. 5:22–23).

When church members evaluate potential deacons to determine if they are acceptable to the church for the role of deacon, they should not be judgmental. They should be aware that the standard by which deacons are measured is the same used to measure themselves. The high expectations that the church has of its deacons are no more than God expects of all Christians.

Confidence for Ministry

By this time the readers of Paul's deacon qualifications and of this book may despair, "Could anyone qualify to be a deacon?" The reader might also ask, "If any could measure up to those high expectations, wouldn't they be justifiably proud of that achievement?"

Pride and boasting are condemned in both the Old Testament and the New Testament. Jesus told the parable of the Pharisee who prayed publicly, "God, I thank You that I'm not like other people"; and a tax collector who quietly prayed, "O God, turn your wrath from me—a sinner!" Jesus concluded, "Everyone who exalts himself will be humbled, but the one who humbles himself will be exalted" (Luke 18:9–14). By their very role of being servants, deacons will not seek to lift themselves up but to serve where needed.

The result of being accepted by God and the church is not pride but confidence. Paul concluded his section on deacon qualifications by speaking of those already serving. "Those who have served well as deacons acquire a good standing for themselves, and great boldness in the faith that is in Christ Jesus" (1 Tim. 3:13).

Matthew concluded Jesus' Sermon on the Mount with the comment, "When Jesus had finished this sermon, the crowds were astonished at His teaching. For He was teaching them like one who had authority, and not like their scribes" (Matt. 7:28–29). Jesus had such a confidence that he did not need to assert his authority over others. Instead he expressed his confident leadership through service and giving his life for others (Mark 10:45).

The Holy Spirit's power changed the Twelve from denying, running, and hiding disciples into confident leaders. They were willing to risk their lives to preach God's Word boldly. Even the Jewish council recognized the confidence of Peter and John (Acts 4:13). The council tried to stop their ministry with threats. However, when Peter and John returned to their Christian friends, they prayed, "Lord, consider their threats and enable your servants to speak your word with great boldness" (Acts 4:29 NIV). When they finished praying, "the place where they were meeting was shaken. And they were all filled with the Holy Spirit and spoke the word of God boldly" (Acts 4:31 NIV). The word translated "boldness" here is the same word used for the confidence of deacons in 1 Timothy 3:13. The result of such boldness and confidence in the early church was unity of the congregation, witnessing with power, and sharing possessions with those in need (Acts 4:32–35).

Stephen, one of the seven leaders chosen to minister to the Greek-speaking widows, spoke with such boldness that the leaders of the synagogues "were unable to stand up against the wisdom and the Spirit by whom he spoke" (Acts 6:10). He had such inner confidence that he was able to go to his death with a prayer of forgiveness for those who were stoning him (Acts 7:60).

Deacons who serve with confidence "acquire a good standing" in the congregation. This is not a status that lifts them above the other church members. It is a profound respect by the church members for deacons who have been their servant models. Church members appreciate their deacons for demonstrating and encouraging growth toward mature faith, Christian family life, personal and public morality, and ministry that is acceptable and pleasing to God.

CHAPTER 6

Deacons Model
Ministry as Partners

IT IS TIME TO STAMP OUT pastor-deacon jokes. Most pastor-deacon jokes make fun of pastor-deacon conflict. For the most part, those jokes are not true. Most pastors and deacons have healthy relationships.

Usually a pastor looks to deacons with a great deal of fondness. The pastor appreciates the significant role deacons have played in developing his ministry, his life, and his leadership style. Deacons loved their pastor enough to give support and encouragement when he was discouraged. When people were not responding the way the pastor had hoped, a deacon would help his pastor discover more realistic expectations and help him sort through what was happening. Sometimes a deacon would lovingly help the pastor be aware of some things he had done poorly. The deacon was not attacking his pastor but was helping him see other ways to be more effective. Pastors often look to such deacons as those who have been the primary shaping influence for good in their ministry.

Also, most deacons look to their pastors with a great deal of fondness and appreciation for how they have helped them grow in Christ and cared for them and their families in times of crisis. They take seriously what Paul wrote: "The elders [pastors] who direct the affairs of the church well are worthy of double honor, especially those whose work is preaching and teaching" (1 Tim. 5:17 NIV). Deacons with this perspective acknowledge and value the distinctive leadership role God has given their pastor.

For the most part, all those pastor-deacon jokes that play on conflict are simply not true. However, sometimes the conflict between the pastor and deacons does exist. But such conflict is no joke. It is tragic and painful, and it ought not to be joked about. Instead of laughing about conflict, pastors and deacons can work at developing a team relationship.

In order to build a relationship as partners, pastors and deacons need:

- to drop their defenses and knock down the barriers,
- to study Scripture that teaches about biblical leadership and about partnership, and
- to reexamine interpretations of Scripture that have created incorrect distinctions between the pastor and deacons. Such distinctions have often resulted in barriers between these two church leadership roles rather than partnership and teamwork.

Sharing Ministry with the Pastor

The New Testament model of service points to deacons serving alongside the pastor in pastoral ministries. Ernest Mosley wrote: "As team leader, the pastor is responsible for equipping deacons for their ministry and drawing on all the resources available to them for training in order that they may be able to minister with increasing effectiveness. He will guide the deacons in discovering and performing their responsibilities."[1]

As partners with the pastor, deacons have the privilege and opportunity to share in modeling ministry to the church. Chapters 7 through 9 suggest some ways deacons can be examples to the congregation as they carry out their duties of caring for families, proclaiming the gospel, and leading the church.

How can the pastor and deacons work together to create a positive relationship as partners? How can they set the example for shared ministry throughout the congregation?

They can begin by following the example of Jesus as a servant leader. The pastor will not need to demand followship. He will not try to push or pull the church toward its goals. Rather, he will lead by his character, his example, and his vision. The deacons will give up their need to run the church as a controlling board. They will seek ways to be released from managing the business of the church. This isn't because the business of the church is unspiritual or less important but because the deacons need to focus on broader ministries.

If the pastor and deacons are to form a meaningful partnership, the pastor needs to be willing to share his ministry rather than try to be the only minister and maintain control. He will respect the deacons and have confidence in their ability to carry out their responsibilities. Of course, the deacons must be willing to accept ministry without trying to grab power. We recognize that God's work cannot be done single-handedly. There are no solo performances in the kingdom of God.

The pastor and deacons will avoid unbiblical styles of relating. The pastor will refuse to assume the role of the chief executive officer of the corporation with the deacons being volunteer staff to carry out his directions. The deacons will reject the role of the board of directors who are ultimately in charge of running everything, including telling the pastor what to do. Instead they will adopt the biblical pattern of mutual submission under the lordship of Christ.

Finally, the pastor must be responsible to equip the deacons for their ministry tasks (Eph. 4:12). And the deacons must be willing and available to be trained as partners in ministry. Studying this book together is a positive way for deacons to redefine and renew their energy for this shared ministry.

Paul wrote, "We are God's co-workers" (1 Cor. 3:9). Surely the pastor and deacons, as leaders of the church, ought to be laborers together, partners with each other as they share God's work. When the pastor and deacons develop this kind of shared ministry, they will be setting an example of Christian unity for all Christians.

The deacons share leadership with the pastor and other staff in the work of the church as they all carry out their distinctive roles and functions. Deacons also can encourage and work with existing church organizations, leaders, and ministries. When deacons recognize and affirm the spiritual gifts and value of all church members, they will think in terms of shared ministry and leadership. They will find a variety of practical ways to share the work of leading, proclaiming, and caring.

To have this team relationship, a relationship as partners, the pastor and deacons first need a relationship of love. Love means wanting God's best for other persons. Those who love others will spend time building them up, not tearing them down. Those who love will not be content with letting them be less than God intends.

Sometimes a well-intentioned deacon tries to help the pastor, but the pastor does not want the offered assistance. That rejection hurts because the deacon loves the pastor and wants to help him in a healthy way. On the other hand, sometimes the pastor tries to help the deacons, but the deacons will not be helped. That situation is painful to the pastor because he loves the deacons and wants to help them grow.

Not only do we recognize that this partnership—this team relationship—must be based on a relationship of love, but we also recognize that it must be based on a relationship of equals. In the church, all people are equal before God. The church belongs to God. As head of the church, all lordship and authority belong to Christ. In his description of the church as the body of Christ, Paul emphasizes that all members of the church are essential to the proper functioning of the body. He allows no room for attitudes of superiority (1 Cor. 12:21) or inferiority (1 Cor. 12:15–16).

To say all are equal under God and every Christian is a minister is sometimes confusing to both the pastor and the people. They say: "Where does that leave the pastor? If everyone is equal, he will no longer have a unique position." But that is not true. What is the unique role of the pastor? The word *pastor* means "shepherd" (Acts 20:28; Eph. 4:11; 1 Pet. 5:2). The word *bishop* means "overseer" (Acts 20:28; Phil. 1:1; 1 Tim. 3:1; Titus 1:7; 1 Pet. 5:3). A third term, *elder,* is used interchangeably with the pastor/shepherd and overseer roles (Acts 20:17, 28; 1 Pet. 5:1–3). These titles speak of a definite leadership role. But that role is not in rank; it is in function. The leadership function of the pastor/overseer/elder is to equip and enable the rest of the congregation to do their work of ministry (Eph. 4:12).

The word *deacon* appears in our English Bible in only two passages. In Philippians 1:1, Paul greeted the church at Philippi and specifically greeted the overseers and the deacons. Paul gave the qualifications, first of the overseers and then of the deacons, in 1 Timothy 3. However, the word *diakonos,* which is translated "deacon" in those two Scripture passages, appears in that form and its related forms over one hundred times in the New Testament (see Appendix). Usually it is translated either "servant" or "minister," "service" or "ministry," or "to serve" or "to minister." Only in these two passages did the translators choose not to translate it but to create a new word. This was first done with the Latin translation as early as the fourth century.

Since in both passages Paul used *diakonos* in association with the leadership role of the overseers (pastors), he seemed to be referring to a distinctive leadership role in the church. Thus it seemed appropriate to transliterate *diakonos* (changing the *i* to an *e* and the *k* to a *c* and dropping the *os* ending), thereby creating a new word, *deacon,* rather than to use the general term *servant* or *minister.* Apparently as the number of believers increased and new churches were begun, God led the congregations to formalize the servant role into a more specific church leadership role.

The New Testament does not give a specific written job description for deacons. However, the job description is in the very name itself—deacons are to be servants. They are to be ministers working alongside the pastor/overseer.

Rediscovering the Deacon as a Servant

At times in church history deacons have lost sight of their primary function of service. In the book *The Emerging Role of Deacons,* Charles Deweese gives a thorough account of the changing understanding of deacon ministry through the centuries.[2]

During the early centuries of the church's life, deacons understood their work to be primarily practical service. Their ministry included visiting the sick, administering the benevolence funds, providing pastoral care and preventive church discipline, assisting in the Lord's Supper and worship, and training new converts.

Deacons in the Middle Ages from A.D. 500 to 1500 focused their work on worship. The primary reason the servant function of the deacon diminished during this period was that the role of deacon became the first stage toward the priesthood. Instead of the church roles being only distinctive in function, they became different levels or grades of ministry. This led to the sharp distinction between clergy and laity. One other factor in the loss of the deacon's ministry role was the rise of monastic orders that assumed responsibility for practical caring service.

A restudy of the New Testament by the Reformers in the sixteenth century led to the rediscovery of the deacon as a servant. Both Martin Luther and John Calvin emphasized the deacon's role in distributing the church's aid to the poor.

Early Baptist deacons in England and America served as church officers. They were general servants of God, the church, and the needy. They assisted in limited administrative responsibilities.

A greater involvement in business functions began to emerge in the late 1700s and continued into the twentieth century. This led to the concept of deacons as church business managers, acting as a board of directors. As a board of directors, deacons screened all major recommendations to determine whether they should go to the congregation. They controlled the finances, facilities, and other business affairs of the church. The pastor was directly responsible to the deacons rather than to the church.

This view of deacons as church business managers tended to distract from the other areas of service previously given strong attention. Statements such as these began to appear in church minutes and other writings: "Deacons, along with other church officers, are the chief managers of the church." "The duty of deacon is to take care of the secular concerns of a church." "The office of deacon is to relieve the minister from the secular concerns of the church." "A deacon's office extends only to the secular affairs of the church."

In 1846, R. B. C. Howell published one of the most detailed books written on Baptist deacons up to that time. In this book *The Deaconship*, Howell identified the Twelve with the pastor and the Seven with the deacons. He designated deacons as the "financial officers of the church"[3] and referred to them as "a board of officers, or the executive board of the church."[4] Based on his interpretation of Acts 6, he assigned the temporal department of the church to the deacons and the spiritual department to the pastor.[5] Howell's book was popular and has had a continuing influence on Baptist deacons.

Howell's interpretation of Acts 6 and the role of deacons was continued by Prince E. Burroughs in his book *Honoring the Deaconship*. Published by the Sunday School Board (now LifeWay Christian Resources) of the Southern Baptist Convention, this book was the official deacon study book from 1929 to 1956. Burroughs wrote, "As the apostles were forerunners of the pastors who later served the churches in a distinctly spiritual capacity, so these men [the Seven] were beyond doubt the forerunners of the deacons who later came to serve the churches in material affairs."[6]

Burroughs went on to say, "In the division of labor and the assignment of a place to the deacon, a fairly clear line was drawn as to the relation of the deacon to the church. On one side of the line stands the pastor. He is, shall we say, the ranking officer especially entrusted with the ministry which is more distinctly spiritual. On the other side is the deacon, standing next to the pastor, and entrusted with the care of the material interests of the church. He is to care for the properties of the church, its building, its pastor's home, and its other material holdings. He is to direct and safeguard the financial side of its ministry."[7] Obviously, this book had a profound influence on the work of deacons in Baptist churches in the twentieth century.

In the last half of the 1800s and through the 1900s, some church leaders questioned this limited scope of deacon ministry. These leaders cautioned against the misuse of authority by deacons and warned that the board concept violated Baptist church polity. The board approach may be appropriate for the business world but not for Baptist churches committed to congregational decision making.

In *The Baptist Deacon,* released in 1955, Robert Naylor warned that among the deacons in many churches a certain "'bossism' has developed. There is a 'board' complex and a general feeling that deacons are 'directors' of the church. Nothing could be farther from the Baptist genius or the New Testament plan."[8] However, Naylor continued to assume that deacons were business managers. Thus, he sent mixed signals to the deacons who read his book.[9]

An increasing number of church leaders frowned on the heavy involvement of deacons in church business and emphasized that deacons have spiritual duties. In the late 1950s and early 1960s Howard Foshee led in an intensive deacon study. The result was his book *The Ministry of the Deacon,* published in 1968, that has had a profound influence in helping deacons rediscover their work as servants.

Foshee not only reacted against the concept of deacons as a board of directors, but he also opposed the idea of deacons whose sole duties are the management of business matters. He wrote that deacons function in this limited way when they administer church affairs basically as a business operation, when their image is that of decision makers in all business affairs, and when business efficiency is a higher priority than Christian growth and service.[10] In less than two decades, this book became a major factor in changing the deeply ingrained perception of deacons as business managers who run the church to a perception of deacons as ministers in partnership with the pastor.

A popular view has been to trace the origin of deacons to the events recorded in Acts 6:1–7. However, The Acts 6 account does not specifically call the Seven "deacons." In fact, Luke used the same Greek word for "serve *(diakonein)* tables" and for the "ministry *(diakonia)* of the word" (6:2, 4 NASB). Howell, Burroughs, and others misinterpreted Acts 6 and thus developed a wrong job description for deacons.

In focusing on the problem of neglect in this passage, readers often overlook the important fact that the church was taking care of those in the congregation who had need (Acts 2:45; 4:34–35; 6:1). The Christians continued the Jewish custom of making special provision for widows (see Deut. 14:29; 24:19–21).

The Twelve, the apostles, were the only church leaders the early church had to that point. Luke records in Acts 2 and 4 that the people would sell land and other possessions and bring the proceeds to the apostles. The Twelve assumed responsibility for distributing the funds to those in need. This organization apparently worked fine until the problem surfaced that some widows were being neglected. The growth of the church had outstripped its organization for adequate care.

The increasing number of new Christians (Acts 2:41; 4:4; 5:14; 6:1) included Jews from other areas called Hellenists, who either spoke Greek rather than Aramaic or had adopted Greek customs. Possibly the native Hebrews felt resentment and prejudice toward these kinsmen because they felt the Hellenists had compromised with their Gentile culture, or the neglect may have been the result of a communication problem.

Even though the church was a caring congregation, these prejudices or communication problems led to discrimination against the widows of the Hellenists. Such discrimination had the potential to destroy the unity of fellowship that had been so evident in the Christian community (see Acts 2:1, 46; 4:32).

Luke wrote in Acts 6:1–4: "Now at this time while the disciples were increasing in number, a complaint arose on the part of the Hellenistic Jews against the native Hebrews, because their widows were being overlooked in the daily *serving* of food. And the twelve summoned the congregation of the disciples and said, 'It is not desirable for us to neglect the word of God in order to *serve* tables. But select from among you, brethren, seven men of good reputation, full of the Spirit and of wisdom, whom we may put in charge of this task. But we will devote ourselves to prayer, and to the *ministry* of the word'" (NASB, italics added).

The Twelve called the congregation together to deal with the problem. They were apparently willing to demonstrate that the discrimination was wrong by serving the Hellenistic widows themselves. However, this additional caring would have interfered with the priority of their preaching and teaching ministry. They suggested that the church expand the number of church leaders by choosing seven highly qualified men to be responsible for the task. The Jerusalem congregation chose seven new leaders with Greek names, apparently all from the Hellenistic Christian group, to care for the Greek-speaking widows in order to prevent the apostles from being overloaded with those responsibilities.

Notice that three times Luke and the apostles use the same Greek term from which we get our English word *deacon*. In verse 1 it is translated "serving." In verse 2 it is translated "to serve." Both uses refer to the distribution of money or food to help the needy of the congregation. In verse 4 the term is translated "ministry," referring to the proclamation of the Word of God. The Twelve could use the same term interchangeably to refer to preaching the gospel and providing practical care for the needy. They saw these as two sides of the ministry coin and very naturally saw both as inseparable parts of their leadership. They had learned this lesson by observing Jesus.

By meeting the needs of those who had felt neglected, these seven new leaders helped heal a possible break in the church fellowship. Thus, "the preaching about God flourished, and the number of the disciples in Jerusalem multiplied greatly" (Acts 6:7).

Luke does not indicate that the church made the sharp distinction between the function of the Twelve and the Seven stated so strongly by Howell and Burroughs. The rest of Acts 6 through chapter 8 records the action of two of the Seven, Stephen and Philip. Although they had a specific caring ministry to perform, they also were proclaimers of the gospel. The Seven were for the Hellenists what the Twelve were for the Hebrews. Stephen and Philip debated in the Hellenistic synagogues, preached the gospel, and baptized new believers. The Seven had learned from observing the Twelve that preaching the gospel and providing practical care for the needy were inseparable parts of their leadership.

Howell and Burroughs interpret the Twelve as saying, in effect, "We will no longer be involved in serving tables at all. The Seven will serve the needy, and we will preach the gospel." That interpretation requires that the verses be read without considering the total context.

However, the broader context requires us to interpret the Twelve as saying, "If we continue to expand the serving (*diakonein*) tables dimension of our ministry to include the neglected Hellenistic widows, it will upset the balance and make serious inroads into our ministry (*diakonia*) of the Word. That is not wise. So we suggest that we expand the organization by choosing seven additional leaders." The congregation chose seven new leaders to serve the

Hellenistic widows since the Twelve were not giving up their distribution responsibilities for the Hebrew widows.

The Acts 6–8 account never refers to the Seven as "deacons." Later when Paul met Philip in Caesarea on his third missionary journey, Luke identified him, not as a deacon, but as "Philip the evangelist, who was one of the Seven" (Acts 21:8). Not until late in the second century did some in the church associate the Seven with the role of deacons.

Also there is nothing in this passage to justify dividing the church into two different departments—the spiritual and the secular or temporal. How can the money given as tithes and offerings to the Lord be called secular as opposed to spiritual? How can the properties built and dedicated for the purpose of God's kingdom be called temporal as opposed to spiritual? That is an artificial distinction that is foreign to the New Testament. The events recorded in Acts 6 describe a partnership of servant leaders to meet needs, not a division into separate departments.

Such a division is more a reflection of the historical development of the distinction between clergy and laity. That separation is also foreign to the New Testament.

The word *laity* comes from the Greek word *laos,* which means "people" and usually is used in the phrase "the people of God" or "God's people." Thus the *laos,* the people, the laity includes church leaders such as pastors. However, the common definition of layperson is one who is untrained, an amateur, in some way inferior. There is a Greek word with that definition *(laikos),* but it is never used in the New Testament. Unfortunately, a definition for an unbiblical word was applied to a biblical word.

Our word *clergy* comes from the Greek word *kleros,* which means "lot" or "portion." In the New Testament this word and its related words are most often translated "heirs" or "inheritance," referring to that given to those who are received into God's family (Gal. 4:7; Eph. 1:11, 18). The word *kleros* includes all God's people and not just the leaders called pastors.

When Paul referred to the overseers and deacons in greeting the church at Philippi and placed the qualifications for overseers and deacons one after the other in 1 Timothy 3, he gave no hint of the sharp division suggested by Howell and Burroughs. Divisions between spiritual and temporal, between clergy and laity, between pastor and deacons create disunity and conflict rather than the spirit of unity, partnership, and shared ministry emphasized throughout the New Testament.

Organizing for Deacon Ministry

Deacons need to organize themselves to accomplish their tasks. The best organizational structure for deacons in any church is the one that works most effectively.

The deacon body should elect only the officers it needs. For example, it may be that the deacon chairman can keep adequate records and thus a secretary is not needed. Or if the only job for the vice chairman or associate chairman is to preside over a deacons' meeting in the absence of the chairman, that position is probably not needed. Those rare times when the chairman must be absent, any of the other deacons could be asked to preside. Many responsibilities can be handled better by one person serving as a coordinator than by several persons on a committee. Some tasks can be assigned to a temporary coordinator or committee.

A small church may elect only a chairman. A larger church with more deacons will require additional officers. These could include an associate chairman, a secretary, and other associates to coordinate such areas as training, team ministry, family ministry, or other areas of ministry.

Writing out the duties for each officer or committee reveals whether that position is really needed. It also avoids overlapping of responsibilities or neglecting work assigned by the church. And it guides the person holding the position in accomplishing the assigned tasks.

The election of deacon officers is best done just prior to the year they will serve. This approach has two distinct advantages. There is no delay at the beginning of the new year waiting for the officers to be elected. Also only deacons with at least one year of deacon service will be elected. Deacons should prayerfully seek the Holy Spirit's guidance in electing the most qualified persons to lead them.

Some churches have renamed the associate or vice chairman "chairman-elect." That means this person will become the chairman the following year. This assures a smooth transition in leadership and provides time for extra training and preparation. The chairman-elect could also meet with the church leadership team as it makes plans for the following church year.

The Deacon Chairman

The chairman of deacons is more than a presiding officer. The deacon chairman is one of the most important places of leadership in the church. He is a spiritual leader who has the opportunity to lead the deacons to fulfill their mission in the total area of deacon ministry. The position provides a unique opportunity to work closely with the pastor. The two can build a special relationship of partnership, appreciation, encouragement, and support.

The chairman's leadership style should be consistent with Jesus' instructions to his disciples. "You know that those who are regarded as rulers of the Gentiles dominate them, and their men of high positions exercise power over them. But it must not be like that among you. On the contrary, whoever wants to become great among you must be your servant, and whoever wants to be first among you must be a slave to all" (Mark 10:42–44).

The duties for the deacon chairman could include:

- Coordinate with the pastor the work of the church's deacon ministry.
- Lead the deacons in planning, conducting, and evaluating all of their work.
- Plan, conduct, and evaluate deacons' meetings.
- Provide deacons with adequate training and resources for their work.
- Guide deacons in organizing and conducting a ministry to families in the church.
- Serve as a member of the church leadership team to interpret deacon work to the team and to provide deacons with information about the total work of the church.
- Report regularly to the church on the work of the deacons.
- Give guidance to the pastoral ministries of the church when it is without a pastor.

The Associate Chairman

The associate or vice chairman should be given responsibilities that can justify the existence of that position. Some churches assign coordination of deacon training or coordination of family ministry to this position.

The duties for the associate chairman could include:

- Assist the chairman in planning, conducting, and evaluating deacon work.
- Serve as moderator for deacons' meetings in the absence of the chairman.
- Coordinate preparation for the Lord's Supper, if this responsibility is not assigned to a church committee.

- Be responsible for other specifically assigned tasks.

The Deacon Secretary

The duties for the deacon secretary could include:
- Keep accurate minutes and records of deacon work.
- Prepare deacon ministry reports.
- Prepare and revise notebooks for deacons' use in family ministry.
- Order and maintain a supply of deacon ministry materials for deacons to use in their work.

The Training Associate

The duties for the training associate or coordinator could include:
- Provide training events and opportunities for training in deacon ministry for deacons, pastor, church staff, and deacons' wives. These include group and individual study; church deacon retreats; and participating in associational, state, and national deacon ministry conferences.
- Keep records of deacon ministry training.
- Work with the church's discipleship leader to provide training opportunities in deacon ministry for all church members.

Team Leader for _____ Ministry

If the deacons are organized into various teams for specific ministries, each team will need a leader. The duties for a team leader could include:
- Coordinate the work of the team's ministry assignment.
- Be the primary contact for the pastor, church staff, or other church members related to the team's assignment.

- Report on the ministry to the deacons and church.

The Family Ministry Associate

If the deacons use the Deacon Family Ministry Plan, the duties for the family ministry associate or coordinator could include:

- Organize family ministry groups and coordinate the Deacon Family Ministry Plan.
- Keep the church aware of the deacons' ministry to families.

Deacons have a great heritage in ministry to persons. Sometimes in the past deacons have lost sight of their servant role, but today deacons are demonstrating a growing excitement as they have opportunity to share ministry with their pastor. With adequate organization and preparation, deacons can effectively model ministry as partners.

CHAPTER 7

Deacons Model
Care for Families

AT THE LAST SUPPER Jesus said these words to his disciples: "I give you a new commandment: that you love one another. Just as I have loved you, you should also love one another. By this all people will know that you are My disciples, if you have love for one another" (John 13:34–35).

Up to this time people could easily know who were the disciples of Jesus. *Disciple* means "follower" or "learner." As Jesus moved about the countryside, people saw those who were following Jesus and recognized them as Jesus' disciples. Jesus was telling his disciples that soon he would not be there to be followed physically. The disciples would then be identified by the way they loved one another with Jesus' kind of love. This continues to be true today. The disciples of Jesus are recognized by their love for one another.

The church has always assumed responsibility to care for the spiritual and physical needs of persons. However, many needs go unmet when church members turn over their caring responsibility to the pastor. Even when church members do accept their part in caring, some people may still miss out on the care that is available in the congregation. The problem is that everybody's business is nobody's business. Although many people receive adequate care, some do not. Everyone assumes that someone else is meeting that need.

Every church should be known by its love. If there were a church with no love, all the people would leave and the church would cease to exist. However, in any loving church a person could be found that had been significantly associated with the church who might say: "That church! I wouldn't have anything to do with that church. They don't care for anybody!" What happened? That person did not receive the love and care that was available in that congregation at some key point in life. That is always a tragedy.

Many churches turn to their deacons for help in meeting the needs of church members. Assigning each church family to a deacon is a simple and effective approach to reduce the possibility that some members will be neglected. Some churches have a deacon of the week to visit the sick and shut-ins and to be on call to work with the pastor in meeting needs. Other churches have deacon teams to meet various specific needs.

When deacons focus their attention on administrative duties, they often fail to emphasize their caring responsibilities adequately. In some churches deacons are able to carry on coordinating and other leadership duties and still care for families effectively in the congregation, but others have found it more helpful to release some of their specific duties to church committees and their coordinating responsibility to the church leadership team.

Caring as Jesus Cared

Jesus told his disciples that he was washing their feet as an example for them to follow. No task was too menial for those who would serve as Jesus served (John 13:12–16). With Jesus as a clear model, Christians may answer Cain's question, "Am I my brother's keeper?" (Gen. 4:9 NASB) with a resounding yes!

John wrote that Christ demonstrated love by giving his life for us. We are to do the same for others. Our love cannot be "just words or talk; it must be true love, which shows itself in action" (1 John 3:18 GNB). John stated that if we have the resources to meet a person's need and turn away, we cannot claim to have God's love (1 John 3:17).

James went so far as to say that faith which is not expressed in the practical works of meeting physical needs is dead, useless, and cannot save (James 2:14–17). In this spirit Paul declared that Christian brothers are to "carry one another's burdens; in this way you will fulfill the law of Christ" (Gal. 6:2).

In Jesus' parable of the last judgment, he divided people into those who are worthy and those who are unworthy to inherit the Father's kingdom. Jesus based this division on acts of mercy toward those who have needs. "Come, you who are blessed by My Father, inherit the kingdom prepared for you from the foundation of the world. For I was hungry and you gave Me something to eat; I was thirsty and you gave Me something to drink; I was a stranger and you took Me in; I was naked and you clothed Me; I was sick and you took care of Me; I was in prison and you visited Me. . . . Whatever you did for one of the least of these brothers of Mine, you did for Me" (Matt. 25:34–36, 40). Those welcomed into the kingdom were surprised since they had not related their acts of mercy to Christ. They had acted in response to human need, not for reward.

When asked what commandment was the greatest, Jesus combined two inseparable commands—love God and love your neighbor as yourself (Mark 12:28–31). In a similar encounter recorded in Luke (10:25–37), a lawyer asked Jesus, "Who is my neighbor?" The parable of the good Samaritan was not really an answer to that question but to the rephrased question Jesus asked after telling the parable. "Who proved to be a neighbor and thus showed he loved his neighbor as himself?"

Christian love is a decisive act, seeking the best interests of the person loved. The Samaritan had done this beyond any expected sense of duty. He was generous with his resources. He cleaned and bandaged the stranger's wounds, used his beast to carry him to the inn, cared for him overnight, and accepted financial responsibility for his continued care. The Samaritan remains an example of generous care for a person in need.

Jesus modeled this care. He "went about doing good" (Acts 10:38). Jesus identified himself as the Good Shepherd who laid down his life for his sheep (John 10:11). When he saw the multitude who were like sheep without a shepherd, he felt compassion for them. He knew he was not to do it all himself. He needed coworkers to care for the flock. He asked his disciples to pray that additional workers would be sent (Matt. 9:36–38). The disciples' prayers were answered as they were sent to carry Jesus' teaching and healing ministry to the lost (Matt. 10:5–8).

As Jesus commissioned the disciples as partners in his caring ministry, deacons can be partners with their pastor in caring for people. Deacons will naturally feel inadequate, but that inadequacy leads to a healthy dependence on God's strength. Jesus promised, "The one who believes in Me will also do the works that I do. And he will do greater works than these, because I am going to the Father. Whatever you ask in My name, I will do it, so that the Father may be glorified in the Son. . . . I will ask the Father, and He will give you another Counselor to be with you forever" (John 14:12–13, 16). With the power of the presence of God's Holy Spirit, deacons can be effective partners with God and the pastor (1 Cor. 3:9) in caring for families.

Some persons struggle with their motives for caring. A sense of obligation to meet the expectations of God and others seems to compete with the desire to care "just because

I want to." People also feel the pressure of owing persons who have given them care. Thus, the caring person fears that those who receive his care will feel indebted to him.

The cultural concept of duty, obligation, or responsibility is often based on a fear of failure to live up to the expectations of God and others. But the Christian concept of obedience, care, and mutual responsibility is based on a loving response to a loving God who challenges yet forgives and accepts persons even in their failure. The kind of love and care we have received from God is the kind we are to give because we love our neighbors.

The obligation to care can become legalistic or can be in response to the fear of losing a relationship. But obligation and mutual responsibility can be expressions of a loving, caring relationship if there is a consistency between what a person feels he is supposed to do and what he wants to do. Caring for others is rooted in a deacon's relationship with God in Christ.

Organizing for Caring Ministry

A spirit of Christian fellowship is probably a church's most valuable resource. Such fellowship will attract people even when buildings, budget, and leadership are inadequate. People are drawn to a caring church where Christian love is demonstrated through attitudes and actions. Deacons can organize themselves in ways to be sure that people experience that love.

Deacon Welcoming Ministry

One way deacons can build such a climate is to make both members and nonmembers feel welcome when they attend the services. Words of greeting and warm handshakes contribute to a sense of togetherness. Every visitor is a potential new Christian and/or member. Immediate follow-up is crucial. In some churches the deacons take turns on Sunday afternoons visiting those who were visitors in the worship service that morning. People usually respond positively to such a clear indication that they are important to the members of the church.

Deacon Team Ministry

Another way to organize for caring ministry is to divide the deacons among various deacon ministry teams to meet specific needs. Deacons can choose to serve on a team based on their spiritual gifts, abilities, and experiences. "The participating deacons perform more as care *specialists* than care *generalists*. This helps some deacons to more faithfully perform ministry."[1]

The deacons will customize their team ministry based on the congregation's needs. Each team will need a clear description of responsibilities. In some churches the deacon team enlists other church members to be involved in carrying out the team's assignment. The following are a few examples of deacon ministry teams:

A *New Member Ministry Team* is a natural channel for welcoming and assimilating new families as they join the church. Within a few days after they join, an assigned deacon can visit in the home. The deacon can share a packet of materials to acquaint the family with the church and its ministries and to enlist them in Bible study and in new church member activities. This early personal contact will help them know they have become a part of a caring congregation. Sometimes the deacon is responsible for the new member for an extended period of time.

A *Crisis Ministry Team* can minister to those facing personal or family illness, a death of a family member, separation or divorce, family conflict, and the birth of a child. In a larger church this team may be divided into two or more teams.

An *Evangelism and Outreach Ministry Team* will visit both nonbelievers and believers who have participated in some church activity. The deacons' first concern will be their relationship with God through Christ and then their becoming a part of the church family.

A *Benevolence Ministry Team* develops and implements a plan for responding to a variety of needs that arise that a family cannot handle alone. The team will become familiar with the resources available in the church and community to meet such needs.

A *Homebound Ministry Team* will develop a plan for regular visits to members who are nursing home residents and those who live at home but can no longer attend church activities. This might be called a Shut-in Ministry Team.

A *Community Newcomers Ministry Team* will find ways to reach out to individuals and families moving into the community. Although newcomers will appreciate information about how to find basic services, they also need new friends and spiritual guidance during a time of transition.

An *Inactive Members Ministry Team* will reach out to those church members who are inactive and those who seem about to become inactive. The team will be encouragers and reconcilers in order to recover these members.

A *Recognitions Ministry Team* can remember special events with a greeting card or phone call. A contact on anniversaries of marriage, baptism, church membership, or other special events will lead people to feel that the church cares enough to remember. Graduations, job promotions, election to organizational offices, athletic awards, academic achievements, community citations—all are times deacons can build the fellowship by acknowledging a person's special recognition.

Deacon Family Ministry

The Deacon Family Ministry Plan provides an organizational handle by which deacons can get hold of their caring ministry. This plan is a simple organizational device that seeks to reduce the possibility that people will fail to receive love and care when they need it. Basically, the plan involves dividing church families into equal groups and assigning a deacon to each group. Each deacon accepts responsibility to see that the assigned families receive the love and care available in the congregation.

Church leaders found this simple approach helpful as early as the third century. Fabian, bishop of Rome (A.D. 236–250), divided the city into districts and assigned each of the deacons one of the districts.[2] In 1928 *The Office of Deacon* by J. T. Henderson was published. Henderson, leader of the Baptist Brotherhood of the South, suggested that "35 members who reside in a definite territory" be assigned to each deacon. He stated that "this general plan of organization is employed with most gratifying results by a large number of churches."[3]

At least since the early 1950s, deacons in an increasing number of churches began shifting their primary responsibilities from management and administration to a variety of practical ministries. As deacons sought to provide caring service to the members, a natural step was to divide the responsibility to make their ministry more effective throughout the entire congregation. Churches used a variety of titles for this ministry such as Deacon Zone Plan, Deacon Family Visitation Program, Deacon Flock Plan, and Deacons' Ministry to the Congregation.

In response to this movement by the churches, the Sunday School Board (now LifeWay Christian Resources) of the Southern Baptist Convention prepared materials under the title Deacon-led Spiritual Growth Program. The name evolved to Deacon-led Spiritual Care Program, Deacon Family Care Plan, and finally to Deacon Family Ministry Plan. This approach to organizing deacons for effective ministry increased rapidly in popularity.

The plan is simple. Each deacon accepts responsibility to minister to the needs of a group, ideally ten to fifteen resident families. The church has a continuing responsibility for nonresident members, but they would not be assigned to deacons. Inactive members may not be assigned but cared for in some other way. Those away temporarily in school or military service could be assigned to deacons. Some deacons may be able to minister effectively to a greater number of persons than other deacons.

The division is often made by geographical location, but any plan that meets the church's needs is appropriate. Each deacon accepts responsibility for personal ministry to the assigned families for a period of time, usually one year or a full deacon term. The plan is not primarily a visitation program, though personal visits are involved. It is a relationship between the deacons of the church and every member of every family in the church.

Often someone questions whether deacons are qualified to minister to families and whether people will accept their ministry. A church member addressed this issue in a letter to her pastor: "When I first heard of the Deacon Family Ministry Plan, I thought, Well, that will be very nice for other people, but if I need spiritual or any other kind of help, I sure won't settle for a deacon. I want the pastor. Last week my deacon called on me. . . . I can't even begin to express my appreciation both to him for taking the time to visit and to you for initiating the plan. Needless to say, my thinking has undergone a drastic overhauling. Now I will gladly call my deacon. . . . Never have I heard of anything done in our church which has been received with such overwhelming enthusiasm."[4]

Not only are the deacons who minister and the families who receive their ministry benefited, but the whole church fellowship is strengthened. A pastor expressed the observation of many: "There is no doubt that our fellowship is much stronger and our members are being ministered to more thoroughly and effectively as a result of the Deacon Family Ministry Plan. The ministry of the staff is being greatly multiplied. The church is being led by its spiritual leaders to see that all Christians are to be ministering, compassionate, serving people."[5]

Deacon Yokefellow Ministry

In some churches deacons enlist yokefellows (helpers or associates) to work with them in ministering to persons. Jesus said, "Take My yoke upon you and learn from Me" (Matt. 11:29). An untrained ox was placed in a yoke with a trained ox in order to teach the younger animal. Being yoked together enables a less experienced person to learn from a more experienced partner. In a yokefellow ministry, each deacon selects a layman as a partner to share the ministry. It is not necessary for the church to elect the yokefellows, and they are not ordained. However, all deacons would submit the names of their yokefellows for approval by the deacon body. In addition to the on-the-job training, yokefellows usually are included in deacon training during the deacons' meetings and at other times.

The yokefellow ministry has a number of advantages. (1) Often a deacon needs a second person to go on visits. (2) It doubles the number of people involved in the deacon ministry to the congregation. (3) This partnership works whether the deacons are serving on ministry teams or have family ministry assignments. (4) The congregation has an opportunity to observe the yokefellows to determine if they would be good candidates to serve as deacons. (5) It provides excellent in-service training for potential deacons. (6) A newer deacon can enlist a deacon who has rotated off the active deacon body as the yokefellow in order to gain from the deacon's greater experience. (7) Those who are ineligible to serve as a deacon (such as minimum age or length of time as a church member) could serve as a yokefellow.

Ministering in Times of Crisis

Deacons who build caring relationships through team ministry or family ministry will find it natural to minister in times of crisis. Family members will see deacons as familiar friends. Thus when a crisis occurs, an individual or family will feel more at ease as a deacon ministers to them.

Our English word *crisis* comes from the Greek word *krisis,* which means "separation" or "decision of a judge." A crisis in a person's life is a turning point, a decisive moment for good or bad. C. W. Brister defines it as "any event or set of circumstances which threatens a person's sense of well-being and interferes with his usual routine."[6]

Thus crises include common developmental events of life such as birth, marriage, and retirement, and more abrupt situational crises such as death, divorce, illness, and family conflict. These experiences change a person's customary pattern of living. Most people are unprepared to make such radical shifts, and thus the change is seen as a crisis.

Alvin Toffler, in *Future Shock,* stated that "there are definite limits to the amount of newness that any individual or group can absorb in a short span of time, regardless of how well integrated the whole may be."[7] Because a person is uncertain about his limits and has a basic fear of the unknown, he tends to be afraid of change.

During such a time of crisis or change, a person is making life-shaping decisions and responses. These can be destructive or constructive. The deacon's goal is to enable the person or family to use such experiences to deepen personal growth and strengthen relationships.

Ministry in times of crisis begins with the deacon's availability and initiative. If a caring relationship is already established, the person in need will often feel the freedom to call for help. Sometimes the person will not reach out even for available help because of intense preoccupation with the situation at hand or thinking, *I hate to bother anyone.* As a representative of the church, a deacon usually has permission to take initiative.

To know when to take initiative requires sensitivity to others. Deacons need to develop the ability to pick up and amplify even faint signals of cries for help. A helpful way to accomplish this is to become more conscious of one's own distress signals.

Often this is more difficult for men than for women since some men are brought up to ignore their feelings. Sidney Jourard concluded from research, "Women, more sensitized to their inner experience, will notice their 'all is not well signals' sooner and more often than men. . . . It is as if women 'amplify' such inner distress signals even when they are dim, while men, as it were, 'tune them out' until they become so strong they can no longer be ignored. . . . Some men are so skilled at dissembling, at 'seeming,' that even their wives will not know when they are lonely, anxious, or hungering for affection. And the men, blocked by pride, dare not disclose their despair or need."[8] Getting in touch with one's own feelings is not easy, but the increased sensitivity to others is worth the effort.

God awakens sensitivity to persons in different ways. Sometimes God makes a deacon aware of a person in need.

Someone's name comes to mind and it can't be turned loose. The deacon calls or visits the person not knowing why. The other person begins to share how much he needed someone right at that time. The person may say, "How did you know?" Well, the deacon did not know but was led by God's Spirit to a divine appointment to meet a need.

More often God leads in more down-to-earth, practical ways. Experience and common sense often are all a deacon needs to be aware that a person needs someone's care. A wife enters the hospital for surgery. A parent dies. A husband and father loses his job. A faithful church member's health forces her to stay at home. A couple announces they are separating. A teenager is arrested. These events signal a need for caring ministry.

A family in crisis needs the strength and confidence that the presence of a stable, faithful Christian can give. The deacon's presence can be emotional first aid.

Usually the greatest fear a deacon has about ministering in a crisis situation is, What will I say? The better question is: How will I listen? Listening is probably one of the most effective ways a deacon can minister. Especially during a crisis, people need someone who actively listens. People need room to express their feelings more than they need explanations or simple answers to difficult questions.

The simple words "I care" and "I love you" backed by practical assistance will strengthen a person's awareness of God's love and care. The deacon can also use prayer and Scripture to draw the person or family to the guiding and strengthening resources of God's presence.

The well-intentioned offer, "Let me know how I can help," often places more burden on the person in crisis. Usually the deacon can see details which need to be done, such as making phone calls, arranging child care, or providing transportation. The purpose of such helping is not to feel useful but to meet real needs. When a deacon encourages individuals and families to handle all they can themselves, that enables them to use and develop their own strength to cope with the crisis. The deacon can especially provide emotional support for the person in the family who is looked to for stability and decisions.

The deacon can also inform and involve the pastor, relatives, and friends who already have significant relationships with family members. However, the deacon must not share confidential information without the person's permission. Also, printed materials can be left for the person to read at a later time.

The caring person will let the direction of the other person's maturity guide and determine the help that is provided. To help another person is to help that person care for himself and become responsible for his own life. Helping people build their own support systems is also an important part of preventive caring.

Persons often need continued ministry after the immediate crisis has subsided. A key to effective follow-up ministry is a good record-keeping system. It is impossible for most people to remember everything they need to remember. Recognizing this, a professor told his students: "Write it down. Paper is cheaper than brains!" Follow-up notes, phone calls, and visits remind the person of the deacon's continued concern and availability.

Two great challenges of care confront all Christians, including deacons. These are the hungry and homeless of the world. These needs are complex, but Christians who read newspaper accounts of starving people and thousands of refugees and displaced people fleeing oppression cannot ignore a sense of compassion and the need to respond. These same Christians read, "If anyone has this world's goods and sees his brother in need but shuts off his compassion from him—how can God's love reside in him?" (1 John 3:17). The statistics are staggering—over thirty million displaced persons and refugees throughout the world and nearly a billion persons with a consistently inadequate diet. Each person can determine how to meet a part of that need such as giving to hunger relief through mission agencies, sponsoring a refugee family, or direct personal involvement.

Sensitive deacons will discover far more needs than they can adequately meet personally. Deacons will be faced with determining priorities. To paraphrase the words of Jesus, "What will it profit a deacon to win the love and appreciation of an entire congregation but neglect his relationship with God and lose his own family." The Holy Spirit will not only provide the strength for caring but will also give guidance in deciding when and how to minister.

CHAPTER 8

Deacons Model
Proclamation of the Gospel

DEACONS WHO ARE CONCERNED for others will be looking for and sensitive to appropriate opportunities to witness to non-Christians. This will be especially true as they build relationships with individuals and families through their deacon ministry. Every deacon will come to know personally children, teenagers, and adults who are related to church members but are not Christians. God can use that personal relationship as a basis for the deacon's natural and effective presentation of the gospel. Contact with families will also provide numerous opportunities to help Christians apply the gospel in their everyday lives.

The Jerusalem church chose seven new leaders to care for the Hellenistic widows and to heal the fellowship. Luke recorded the actions of two of these seven in Acts 6–8. They are seen proclaiming the gospel to crowds of people and to an individual person. These two set a good example for deacons to follow in their task of proclaiming the gospel to believers and unbelievers.

Stephen's powerful ministry attracted considerable attention. He was drawn into debate with some of the Hellenistic Jews. He was able to speak with such clarity and power that the Jews were "unable to stand up against the wisdom and the Spirit by whom he spoke" (Acts 6:10). They resorted to enlisting false witnesses to bring charges to the Sanhedrin, similar to the charges made against Jesus. Stephen refuted the charges from scriptural history, climaxing with Israel's idolatry and rejection of God's prophets. He concluded by confronting the Jewish religious leaders for being as stubborn and resistant to God's leadership as their forefathers had been. The members of the Sanhedrin were enraged, took him out of the city, and stoned him to death. Stephen, the first Christian martyr, died with confidence and hope, asking God's forgiveness of his murderers (Acts 6:11–7:60).

Luke then turned his attention to another of the Seven, Philip. In response to persecution, many of the Christians had to leave Jerusalem but preached wherever they went. Philip preached to responsive crowds in Samaria. Many believed Philip's preaching about the kingdom of God and Jesus Christ and were baptized (Acts 8:5–13). God then led Philip away from a successful ministry to crowds to witness to one person. An Ethiopian official, who had found spiritual truth in the religion of Israel, was returning home after worshiping in Jerusalem. He was reading Isaiah 53 when Philip arrived. When the Ethiopian questioned him about that passage, Philip told him the good news of Jesus. The result was belief, baptism, and rejoicing (Acts 8:26–39). Philip then worked his way up the Mediterranean coast, preaching in each city until he came to Caesarea (Acts 8:40). Philip was known as "the evangelist" when he hosted Paul, who was on his way to Jerusalem at the end of his last missionary journey (Acts 21:8).

Proclaiming as Jesus Proclaimed

Deacons find Jesus to be the primary example for their proclaiming ministry. Jesus declared that preaching the kingdom of God was his primary mission (Luke 4:43). The way he carried out that mission provides a good model for deacons to follow.

Following his baptism and temptation experience, Jesus returned to Galilee where he began his ministry by teaching in the synagogues. In his hometown of Nazareth, he read from the Isaiah scroll a passage that he identified with himself. Jesus knew that God's Spirit had anointed him to announce the Good News and herald the results of that gospel (Luke 4:14–21).

Jesus always focused the content of his preaching and teaching on the kingdom of God, the rule of God in a person's life. However, he communicated that basic message in various ways to meet the need of each individual. Nicodemus was depending on his Hebrew heritage, so Jesus told Nicodemus he needed to be born again spiritually (John 3:1–8). The rich young ruler loved his money, so Jesus asked him to sell all his possessions and give the money to the poor (Mark 10:17–22).

Jesus was willing to cross barriers of social and religious prejudice to give new life in God's kingdom. When he talked to the Samaritan woman at the well, he reached across the barriers of race, religion, sex, and morality (John 4:5–29). The Pharisees questioned why Jesus would go into the homes of tax collectors and sinners who had been rejected by the religiously proud Pharisees. Jesus replied, "Those who are well don't need a doctor, but the sick do" (Matt. 9:10–12).

Without being judgmental Jesus confronted people with the necessity of confessing and turning from their sin. The scribes and Pharisees brought a woman who had been caught in the act of adultery to Jesus for him to confirm a verdict of death by stoning. But Jesus said, "The one without sin among you should be the first to throw a stone at her." When the accusers had left, Jesus said, "Neither do I condemn you. . . . Go, and from now on do not sin any more" (John 8:3–11).

Jesus had an active ministry of teaching, preaching, and healing in many cities and villages. He felt compassion for the masses of people who had such great needs (Matt. 9:35–36), but he recognized the need for regular periods of withdrawal for prayer and rest. He also knew that he could not do all that needed to be done by himself. He told his disciples, "The harvest is abundant, but the workers are few. Therefore, pray to the Lord of the harvest to send out workers into His harvest" (Matt. 9:37–38). The answer to this prayer was the sending of the disciples on a preaching and healing mission to the lost of Israel. They were to proclaim, "The kingdom of heaven has come near" (Matt. 10:5–8).

Sharing Good News with Unbelievers

At the close of his ministry, Jesus commissioned his followers to continue his ministry of proclamation. The Gospels and Acts record different words from Jesus, but all have the same emphasis. On the night of his resurrection, Jesus said simply, "Just as the Father has sent Me, I also send you" (John 20:21). On that night in Jerusalem he interpreted the Scriptures to the disciples. "This is what is written: the Messiah would suffer and rise from the dead the third day, and repentance for forgiveness of sins would be proclaimed in His name to all the nations, beginning at Jerusalem" (Luke 24:46b–47).

Later in Galilee he told them, "Go, therefore, and make disciples of all nations, baptizing them in the name of the Father and of the Son and of the Holy Spirit, teaching them to observe everything I have commanded you. And remember, I am with you always, to the end of the age" (Matt. 28:19–20). Just before his ascension Jesus told his disciples to wait in Jerusalem. "You will receive power when the Holy Spirit has come upon you, and you will be My witnesses in Jerusalem, in all Judea and Samaria, and to the ends of the earth" (Acts 1:8).

Deacons share with all Christians the commission to witness. This means they are to testify to what they have known and experienced personally. Witnesses for Christ tell about Jesus' life and ministry with attention focused on his death and resurrection. But they tell more than facts about Jesus. They point to the life-transforming effects of these events on their own lives. Non-Christians will want to know what difference Christ has made in the life of the witnessing deacon.

Bill Fay cautions, "There is an important difference between loving to reach lost people and loving lost people. A person who loves only the activity will sooner or later lose interest and move on to another activity if he or she has not come to love people as Jesus did."[1]

The hearers determine the credibility of the witnesses by observing the consistency of their lives. How tragic when someone can say, "What you do speaks so loud I can't hear what you are saying." The Jews charged Jesus with blasphemy: "You—being a man—make Yourself God" (John 10:33). Jesus depended on a consistency between his words and works to establish his credibility. "If I am not doing My Father's works, don't believe Me. But if I am doing them and you don't believe Me, believe the works. This way you will know and understand that the Father is in Me and I in the Father" (John 10:37–38).

Witnesses are not responsible for the belief of others but are to remain faithful and true to their testimony. For many Christians that has meant death (see Rev. 6:9; 20:4). Thus the Greek word translated "witness" has become the English word *martyr*. Although martyrdom may not be required of Christians, the spirit of confident and bold witness should be the same whether there is risk or not.

Deacons who are faithful witnesses will experience the thrill of seeing children, teenagers, and adults to whom they have witnessed make their professions of faith in Christ and follow him in baptism.

Deacons also share with all Christians the commission to proclaim the gospel. Two Greek words are most commonly translated "preach" or "proclaim." One means "to herald" or "to announce officially." The other word, taken from the root word meaning "angel" or "messenger," literally means "to bear a good message." The Greek word has become our English word *evangelize*. The evangelist or preacher is one who announces Good News. Jesus never intended for this important task to be limited to pastoral preaching from the pulpit. All Christians are given this commission. They may proclaim the gospel through private conversations, public presentations, or written communications.

Of primary importance in this commission is the content of the Good News proclaimed. It is the same message Jesus preached—the kingdom of God (Luke 9:2). The Good News is that the rule of God is available to provide life as God intended, life in its fullness. The proclaimer, like the witness, focuses attention on Jesus' death and resurrection. The message also includes the necessity of repentance and confession of sin in order to receive God's forgiveness and cleansing and his gift of new life.

Paul wrote to the Corinthians: "Since, in God's wisdom, the world did not know God through wisdom, God was pleased to save those who believe through the foolishness of the message preached" (1 Cor. 1:21). But Paul always kept his preaching in proper perspective. "My speech and my proclamation were not with persuasive words of wisdom, but with a demonstration of the Spirit and power, so that your faith might not be based on men's wisdom but on God's power" (1 Cor. 2:4–5).

Deacons should not excuse themselves from opportunities to preach because they are not good speakers. Moses' protest, "I have never been eloquent . . . for I am slow of speech and slow of tongue" (Exod. 4:10 NASB), angered God because it denied God's power to enable Moses to speak adequately if not eloquently.

Deacons will be given opportunities to proclaim God's message. They are sometimes invited to preach on special occasions such as men's day, deacon ordination, and lay revivals. Deacons can preach on Sundays or Wednesdays when the pastor is sick or away. Sometimes a willing deacon can make the difference between having a good service and having no service at all. Some laymen have led in starting or sustaining a mission. Sometimes they find their varied responsibilities include occasional or regular preaching. Every week many laymen faithfully carry out a preaching ministry in such places as rescue missions, nursing homes, jails, and resort areas. Others proclaim the gospel through Bible studies at work or in their neighborhoods to reach people who are not hearing the gospel preached in a church.

Paul raised the questions: "How can they call on Him in whom they have not believed? And how can they believe without hearing about Him? And how can they hear without a preacher?" (Rom. 10:14). Deacons may not be called to the role of pastor, but often they will be sent by God to preach the Good News of Jesus Christ.

Deacons not only share with all Christians the commission to witness and to preach, but they also have the commission to make disciples. Jesus' followers are expected to go a step further with those to whom they witness and preach. Christians are to make a concerted effort to help others become intimately involved with Jesus.

Disciples are more than passive learners. They choose to have a personal attachment to Christ that shapes life. Jesus expected his disciples to give him priority over self, family, and possessions (Luke 14:26, 33). Paul described this relationship as being "baptized into Christ Jesus" (Rom. 6:3). Jesus spoke of his disciples abiding in him like a branch abides in the vine (John 15:4).

Disciples are those who make up the fellowship of the church (Acts 11:26). Deacons can take that next step beyond witnessing and preaching by encouraging others to become united with Christ's body, the church. Through sharing in the fellowship, study, worship, and proclamation of the church, they will be strengthened in their union with Christ.

Those who proclaim the gospel to unbelievers will not always see the results of their witnessing and preaching. Paul recognized that one person may plant the seed, others may water and nourish, but ultimately God makes possible new life and growth (1 Cor. 3:6–7).

Christ did not limit his commission to reaching only those immediately near us, but included all people of all nations. Deacons demonstrate their commitment to God's commission to world missions through financial support, informed prayer, and direct participation.

Teaching Believers the Christian Way

The Gospel writers emphasized Jesus' teaching ministry as well as his preaching ministry. Preaching is proclaiming the gospel to those who have not heard it or have not received it. Teaching is proclaiming the Christian way of life to those who are already disciples of Jesus Christ. Jesus not only preached the Good News of the kingdom of God but also taught the meaning of God's rule in a person's life to those who believed and were committed to living according to God's will.

The second half of Christ's commission in Galilee was "teaching them to observe everything I have commanded you" (Matt. 28:20). In the Sermon on the Mount, Jesus said that those who keep and teach the commandments would be considered great in God's kingdom (Matt. 5:19).

One of the marks of Christian teaching is constant use of the Bible. Paul wrote Timothy of the value and purpose of God's Word: "From childhood you have known the sacred Scriptures, which are able to instruct you for salvation through faith in Christ Jesus. All Scripture is inspired by God and is profitable for teaching, for rebuking, for correcting, for training in righteousness, so that the man of God may be complete, equipped for every good work" (2 Tim. 3:15–17).

The purpose of Christian teaching based on the Word of God is to instruct believers in the way God intended life to be lived. At times this will involve confronting and rebuking a person living in sin or promoting false doctrines. As uncomfortable as that may be, there are times when people do not need words of comfort but need someone who will speak the word that helps them break through blind spots. This is what Paul called "speaking the truth in love" (Eph. 4:15), and Howard Clinebell called "the growth formula— caring plus confrontation produces growth."[2]

The positive side of teaching is also needed. The word translated "correction" is a combination of two words meaning "praise" or "approval" and "straight" or "upright." This kind of teaching emphasizes restoring a person to the right way through affirmation and encouragement. The writer of Hebrews reminded his readers that the congregational gatherings were important opportunities for "encouraging each another" and to "promote love and good works" (Heb. 10:24–25). Bruce Larson pointed out that "the amazing power of affirmation . . . breaks down our defenses, enables us to admit our guilt, and frees us to relax and let God renew our minds and set our feelings right."[3]

Many deacons teach believers the Christian way through Sunday school, Bible studies, discipleship groups, and missions organizations in their churches. Sometimes deacons counsel persons who make decisions in a worship service. They can help new Christians grow in their faith through encouraging regular personal Bible study and prayer. Deacons can counsel church members seeking to grow spiritually through the application of the gospel to specific problems. They can enrich family life by helping families start or strengthen family worship. And of course, they teach by modeling growth toward mature faith, Christian family life, personal and public morality, and ministry to persons.

Declaring God's Word to the Community

Jesus said that he was sending his disciples into the world but they were not of the world (John 17:14–18). The church is to demonstrate love and concern for the community, but it must not take on the attitudes and morals of the community. Sometimes it is necessary for a church to challenge community standards, policies, and plans. The Old Testament prophets, Jesus, and the apostles were willing to proclaim God's Word against political, economic, social, and religious corruption and oppression. Whenever truth is ignored, freedom is denied, prejudice is encouraged, or justice is obstructed, the people of God should speak out.

Sometimes a deacon will be led by God to speak prophetically. Like Amos, he may not feel trained for that role. Amos said, "I am not a prophet, nor am I the son of a prophet; for I am a herdsman and a grower of sycamore figs. But the Lord took me from following the flock and the

Lord said to me, 'Go prophesy to My people Israel'" (Amos 7:14–15 NASB). Deacons must be sure they are speaking "the word of the Lord" for his purposes and not for their own prejudices or selfish gain. Deacons need to be sensitive to opportunities to make their voices heard at appropriate times and in appropriate ways.

When deacons accept the challenge of sharing the Good News with unbelievers, teaching believers the Christian way, and declaring God's Word to the community, they will recognize their need for growth in knowing and understanding the message God wants them to proclaim. Personal Bible study, Sunday School, and discipleship will become even more important to these deacons. They will also take advantage of special studies on the Bible, specific doctrines, and the issues Christians face. They will seek out skill training in witnessing,* preaching, and teaching. God can greatly use deacons who are willing to model proclamation of the gospel.

---

*4. The following are valuable tools to prepare deacons and others for effective witnessing. *Share Jesus Without Fear* by William Fay and Ralph Hodge (Nashville: LifeWay Press, 1997) uses a series of nonthreatening questions to discover how God is working in a person's life. There is no memorizing since the method relies on the Holy Spirit using the Word of God being read, not quoted. *Evangelism Through the Sunday School: A Journey of FAITH* by Bobby H. Welch (Nashville: LifeWay Press, 1997) explains how Sunday School, as the foundational evangelism strategy in the church "provides the most efficient churchwide evangelism training network to equip members to become passionate soul-winners" (p. 43). The witnessing plan is easy to remember, using the acrostic FAITH.

CHAPTER 9

Deacons Model
Christian Leadership

DEACONS HAVE THE RESPONSIBILITIES of caring for church members and other persons in the community and of proclaiming the gospel to believers and unbelievers. They also share with the pastor the responsibility of leading the church in the achievement of its mission.

Many churches have assigned primarily business management responsibilities to their deacons. This workload tends to dominate the time and energy of deacons. They find themselves unable to fulfill other leading, caring, and proclaiming responsibilities adequately. Thus an increasing number of churches are deciding against having the deacons serve as the business administrators of the church or having them screen committee actions as a church board of directors. Churches are assigning specific responsibilities to appropriate church committees and coordinating responsibilities with the church leadership team. These churches are finding this approach is more likely to assure that families receive adequate care from a loving congregation, that the necessary administration of the church is handled efficiently, and that the Good News of Christ is consistently shared with believers as well as unbelievers.

This shift of responsibility strengthens rather than weakens the leadership role of deacons. They have the broader opportunity to exert powerful and positive leadership in the spirit of humble servants. This type of leadership is expressed with a spirit of unity for the purpose of building a fellowship that both attracts people to a saving relationship with Christ and nurtures them in total discipleship. In this way deacons become positive models of Christian leadership for others in the church. Deacons who take their leadership role seriously can help their church accomplish God's purpose.

Leading as Jesus Led

Leaders will base their style or approach to leadership primarily on the heroes or models they choose. History, literature, business, politics, movies, and television provide a wide variety of heroes to follow. However, many of these are inappropriate examples for those who want to be Christian leaders. Jesus should be the primary model for deacons.

Leaders face the danger of getting carried away with their own importance. Paul encouraged the Philippian Christians, "Do nothing out of rivalry or conceit, but in humility consider others as more important than yourselves" (Phil. 2:3). He then pointed to Jesus as the supreme example of this attitude of humility that is essential to Christian leadership.

Jesus, "existing in the form of God, did not consider equality with God as something to be used for His own advantage. Instead He emptied Himself by assuming the form of a slave, taking on the likeness of men. And when He had come as a man in His external form, He humbled Himself by becoming obedient to the point of death—even to death on a cross. For this reason God also highly exalted Him and gave Him the name that is above every name, so that at the name of Jesus every knee should bow—of those who are in heaven and on earth and under the earth—and every tongue should confess that Jesus Christ is Lord, to the glory of God the Father" (Phil. 2:6–11).

Jesus did not seek to exalt himself. Only God could exalt Jesus in response to his act of humility. He had warned the crowds and his disciples to avoid following the leadership style of their religious leaders who tried to impress others with their prestige and importance. Jesus concluded, "Whoever exalts himself will be humbled, and whoever humbles himself will be exalted" (Matt. 23:12).

Jesus' temptation experience at the beginning of his ministry was basically a struggle with Satan concerning an appropriate style of leadership. He rejected the temptation to turn the stones into bread since he refused to obligate people to follow him by meeting their physical needs. When he did feed the hungry or heal the hurting, it was a sign of God's mercy and not a technique of leadership. Jesus rejected the temptation to jump from the pinnacle of the temple because he refused to presume on God's power. When Jesus did perform signs and miracles, he was being guided by God rather than testing God. He knew that any popular response to his miracle-working power was superficial and thus an inadequate approach to leadership.

Jesus also rejected the temptation to appeal to the people's expectation of a political ruler since he refused to depend on external power and authority. He would not become King of kings and Lord of lords through satanic intrigue and domination but through worshiping and serving God (Matt. 4:1–11).

Jesus felt that the issue of servant leadership was so important that when he came to the close of his ministry, he wanted to drive that message home one more time. The disciples could anticipate that the meal they would later call the Last Supper was something very special to Jesus. Since Jesus had made advance preparations, the disciples would not have been surprised to step through the door to the upper room that night and find every detail had been carefully tended to. Therefore, it was a great surprise that the moment they stepped through the door they saw one glaring omission. "Where is the servant? There is the water and there is the towel, but there is supposed to be a servant to wash our dusty feet before we recline at the table." It never seemed to occur to any of the Twelve that the servant might be one of them.

And so Jesus arose from the table and took off his outer garments because he was about to do a wet, messy job. He performed the menial task of washing the disciples' feet. He washed the disciples' feet one by one. When he came to Peter, Peter was able to blurt out what was surely in the heart of every disciple, a protest that it was inappropriate for Jesus to do that sort of thing. Again, it never seemed to occur to Peter or the others that they could have offered to take his place.

So Jesus completed the task, reclined again at the table, and said these words to his disciples: "Do you know what I have done for you? You call Me Teacher and Lord. This is well said, for I am. So if I, your Lord and Teacher, have washed your feet, you also ought to wash one another's feet. For I have given you an example that you also should do just as I have done for you. I assure you: A slave is not greater than his master, and a messenger is not greater than the one who sent him" (John 13:12–16).

Washing feet is a fairly ordinary, mundane, and trivial activity. It is not very attractive or exciting. But such an attitude of humility or meekness is not low self-esteem. On the contrary, it is disciplined gentleness that grows out of an inner confidence that is a gift from God.

As he introduced the account of the Last Supper, John wrote: "Jesus knew that the Father had given everything into His hands, that He had come from God, and that He was going back to God" (John 13:3). Jesus knew God had given him all authority. Because of his inner confidence, Jesus did not need to assert that authority over others. Gene

Wilkes writes in *Jesus on Leadership:* Jesus "knew that God was in control of his life and ministry. . . . Because God had gifted him with his mission and the abilities to carry it out, he didn't have to worry about losing anything of importance. . . . Jesus knew that his Father in heaven was the source of his mission in life. . . . Jesus was confident . . . that what he was doing was part of his heavenly Father's ultimate plan for his life. . . . He knew who he was, he knew whose he was, and he knew where he was going."[1]

Jesus attracted people to follow him through the strong influence of this leadership style. He was able to get men to quit their jobs to follow him (Matt. 4:18–22; 9:9). Jesus said that some leaders add to the people's burden rather than helping to ease their burden (Matt. 23:4). Jesus attracted people to follow him because he shared their burden. "Come to Me, all you who are weary and burdened, and I will give you rest. Take My yoke upon you and learn from Me, because I am gentle and humble in heart, and you will find rest for your souls. For My yoke is easy and My burden is light" (Matt. 11:28–30). The challenge to follow Christ is attractive because he promised that he will share the yoke and that the yoke he gives is easy to wear because it is life as God intended it to be lived.

Jesus is the deacons' model for Christian leadership. He taught that a leader is able to be "strong without being harsh, gentle without being weak, caring without being sentimental, and forgiving without being spineless."[2]

Leading as Servants

Deacons are church leaders, but they are also to be servants. Sometimes that creates a considerable problem because people think of a leader as someone who is in charge of other people, and of a servant as someone who is somewhere down below helping people. Thus, it is difficult to merge these two concepts and call someone a servant leader. However, that is exactly what a deacon is, a servant leader. It is a seeming contradiction, but Jesus unified the servant and leader roles in his own life and thus modeled servant leadership for us. God expects deacons to be strong, dynamic leaders but always in the spirit of humble servants. As servant models deacons have the opportunity to demonstrate a quality of life and a quality of servant ministry that God would have for every Christian. The deacons set the example.

Jesus had a lot to say to his disciples about being servant leaders. It was a high priority to him. But the disciples had a difficult time understanding this revolutionary style of leadership.

Jesus was trying to prepare his disciples for his arrest and crucifixion. The ninth chapters of both Mark and Luke record a point in his ministry when Jesus decided it was time to share with his disciples that he was going to be arrested, killed, and raised on the third day. The disciples had a hard time understanding that last phrase, "raised on the third day." It was strange enough to them that Jesus would talk about being arrested and killed. Possibly they did not understand because they were preoccupied with something more important to discuss. When they arrived at their destination, Jesus asked them, "What were you arguing about on the way?" They were embarrassed to tell him. Now they would not have been embarrassed to tell him if they had been discussing what he had told them. But they had another agenda. Their agenda was an argument over who among them was the greatest.

When there is an argument over who is the greatest, the real issue is who is going to be least. Most people have long since given up any illusions of grandeur that they are going to be the greatest anything. But just don't let them be least or a part of anything least. Thus they will do all kinds of things to avoid being least. Too often they try to describe things with such comparative words as more or most, better or best. Such words aren't describing anything, only saying what went before was less or worse. This is a part of the desire to be greatest rather that least.

But listen to what Jesus said to his disciples in response to their argument over who was the greatest. "Whoever is least among you all—this one is great" (Luke 9:48). "If anyone wants to be first, he must be last of all and servant of all" (Mark 9:35). That word "servant" is the same word *diakonos* that is translated in those other two passages as "deacon."

In the tenth chapter, Mark records that Jesus again told his disciples that he was going to be arrested, killed, and raised on the third day. In the very next verse Mark records that James and John came to Jesus with a very special request. They would like Jesus to grant that, when he comes in his glory, he would allow them to sit in the positions of honor and prestige and rank, the positions of right and left. The other disciples were very upset—possibly because they hadn't asked first (Mark 10:32–41).

Jesus took this opportunity to contrast clearly between secular and Christian leadership. Jesus called his disciples to himself again and said: "You know that those who are regarded as rulers of the Gentiles dominate them, and their men of high positions exercise power over them. But it must not be like that among you. On the contrary, whoever wants to become great among you must be your servant, and whoever wants to be first among you must be a slave to all. For even the Son of Man did not come to be served, but to serve, and to give His life—a ransom for many" (Mark 10:42–45).

Usually people measure status and prestige by the power to demand service from others. However, Jesus demonstrated that leadership is to be found in becoming a servant of all. Power is discovered in submission and service. The motivation for such service is not to achieve greatness but love of Christ and thus love for his people (John 21:15–17).

Jesus was not abolishing leadership and authority. Lack of leadership would create organizational chaos. On the other hand, Jesus was not just reversing rank by saying that those who have been on top will go to the bottom and those who have been on the bottom will come to the top. Actually, Jesus was abolishing such over/under order, saying that leadership has nothing to do with rank and status and power and prestige. Leadership is strictly a matter of function, and that function is to serve. He was redefining leadership and saying: "Leadership is serving the people. If you want to be a leader, be a servant." Servant leadership focuses not on superiority over others but on partnership and sharing to accomplish what needs to be done.

A leader is someone who has followers. That definition eliminates the autocrat or dictator. It eliminates those who as individuals or as a group would seek to control. They do not have followers; they have subjects. A leader has voluntary followers, those who voluntarily submit to influence but not control. Too often people are tempted to move from allowing leaders appropriate influence to giving them inappropriate control of their lives. That move from influence to control usually begins, not as a power grab by those who would lead, but from people who want to give away their responsibility.

That is a major cause for deacons functioning in the congregation in the role of a controlling board of directors. In some churches when a member is asked what the deacons do, he or she answers, "They run the church."

Howard Foshee suggests three ways to tell that deacons are functioning as a controlling board:

- When all major recommendations from church organizations and church committees are screened by the deacons to determine whether they should go to the congregation.
- When the pastor and staff members are directly responsible to the deacons rather than to the church.
- When the use or expenditure of major church resources, such as facilities and finances, must first be approved by the deacons.[3]

The board role did not begin as a power grab on the part of the deacons. Possibly one hundred and fifty to two hundred years ago a couple of church members came out of a church house, one saying to the other: "Ah, that was tough. I'm not sure I enjoy those business meetings. We have to discuss things that sometimes we differ on and sometimes we argue about. I think it would be great if we just asked the deacons to decide those things and tell us what we ought to do." Thus was founded the board of directors approach to deacon ministry.

There are two problems with the board role for deacons. The first problem is that the people are giving away a responsibility that they have no right to give away. The second problem is the deacons accept that responsibility. I think that the deacons accept that responsibility with good intentions, thinking they are serving the congregation. However, deacons are not really serving their congregation when they accept a controlling board role.

First, when deacons function as a controlling board of directors, they are in direct contradiction to the Baptist way of church government. Baptists have had a strong, historical commitment to congregational decision making. Anyone who has come into life-changing union with Jesus Christ is able to discern from the Lord his will and direction and can make a contribution to the congregation's decision making. Baptists have rejected a type of church government whereby God reveals his will to a congregation through a select group of more spiritual people. When deacons function as a board of directors, they actually are practicing that type of church government. In a Baptist church there is no place for deacons or any other group to function as a controlling board.

For the most part deacons are not trying to grab power when they function as the "board." Church members, willing to relinquish their own responsibility, gave them that role. Because of a commitment to congregational decision making, deacons need to give up that role of running the church.

The second reason that deacons functioning as a board are not really serving their congregation despite their good intention is that controlling is never real servant leadership. As an illustration, my wife and I have two sons. We love our two boys. As they entered the teenage years, we could have said: "The teenage years are difficult years—lots of decisions, lots of opportunities for mistakes. Since we have more adult experience, we will make all of their decisions for them, and thus we will protect them." If we had chosen to do this, what would have been the result? The result would be two young men growing to adulthood incapable of adult decision making. We could have been motivated by love, but we would not have been real servant parents.

The people may be asking the deacons to serve as a board of directors to run the church. They may want them to assume that responsibility, but the deacons are not really being servants to the people. Seeking to protect the church will only keep the members from growing to fuller maturity and responsibility.

Not only will this happen in a group with the deacons functioning as a board, but it can also happen when an individual deacon is ministering to a family. People will always be tempted to give away control of their lives because decision making is hard. When a deacon has served them well, they will come to love, respect, and trust him. Very likely the time will come when they are facing a major decision that they will turn and say: "Please tell me what I should do." Of course, in his wisdom and objectivity he probably has an idea of what they should do. So it would be easy to fall into the trap of saying, "Well, since you asked me, I think this is what you ought to do." This temptation is difficult to resist. When others invite deacons to make decisions for them, they have given the ultimate compliment of trust. The only way to resist that temptation is to have a strong continuing commitment to a servant style of leadership.

Usually what people need is not just making the right decision; it's learning how to make decisions. Deacons can help people in decision making without making the decision for them. That may be the greatest service of all as deacons guide them through a decision-making process. They will do that which is best for the other individual even when it may not be what they are asking the deacons to do for them. And that is a challenge. Jesus would have his leaders to be servants and not controllers. He would want them to use leadership to influence, yes, but not to cross that line to control. Only one deserves control—the Lord Jesus Christ.

Richard Foster suggests a distinction between a willingness to serve and a willingness to be a servant.[4] A person might say: "I am willing to serve, but I want to reserve the right to determine when it is convenient for me to serve. And I am willing to serve, but I want to retain the right to determine how I will serve because some things would not be appropriate for a person like me. And certainly I am willing to serve, but surely you would understand that I would want to reserve the right to determine who I will serve because there are some people that don't deserve to be served."

However, when a person agrees to be a servant, he gives up all of those rights. All who call ourselves by the name of Christ, Christian, have come to that position in the same way by declaring, "Jesus is my Lord." And if Jesus is Lord, what role does that give but to be his servants. That means saying to Jesus, "You have the right to determine when and how and whom I will serve."

A significant problem is a preoccupation with the drive toward success—a drive toward being greater and the greatest. It infects individuals and congregations—wanting to be the biggest in something, anything; the greatest in something, anything. The opposite preoccupation is the avoidance of failure and being least. But success and failure are not even servant words. The servant words are obedience and stewardship. The servant isn't concerned with whether he succeeds or fails. The servant is concerned with whether he is being obedient to the Master in carrying out the assigned task, and whether he is being a good steward of the resources that the Master has placed at his disposal to carry out the assigned task. Obedience and stewardship—these are the servant words.

In the qualifications of deacons in 1 Timothy 3, Paul concluded with these words, "Those who have served well as deacons acquire a good standing for themselves" (3:13). That sounds like what Jesus said: "If you want to be first, be a servant." Paul and Jesus do not say that deacons get high standing, they are elected to be deacons, they become leaders, so then they can serve. Rather, they emphasize that when deacons serve well, those who receive their ministry will give them greatness, leadership, influence, and respect.

Paul continued, deacons also will acquire "great boldness in the faith that is in Christ Jesus" (3:13). This confidence comes because deacons recognize that God is working in their lives to help other people. The fact that the people are giving deacons their respect and love demonstrates that God is working through them. That builds an increasingly growing confidence and boldness so God can use deacons in even greater ways as servants.

Deacons are called to be servant leaders. Every deacon in every church should live up to the name servant.

Serving as Enabling Leaders

Although the pastor as the overall leader of the congregation has a distinctive equipping ministry, deacons are in a unique position to model an enabling style of servant ministry. Every Christian can and should seek to become an enabling person.

Paul wrote that the purpose of Christian leadership is to train God's people "in the work of ministry, to build up the body of Christ." The leader's goal is to enable Christians to grow "into a mature man with a stature measured by Christ's fullness." The leader also equips every member of Christ's body to function properly and thus enables the whole church to grow "in love" (Eph. 4:12–16).

When church members respect and trust their leaders, they accept their influence. Church members respect deacons who are dedicated Christians, caring ministers, and enthusiastic supporters of the church. They will trust deacons who show love and acceptance, keep confidences, meet their needs, and impress them as genuine. Church members will respect leaders who demonstrate humble confidence and boldness based on a trust in God's power available to all his people. They will reject leaders who display arrogant confidence based on a sense of possessing power in ways not available to others.

Deacons exercise their enabling leadership by helping members discover opportunities to develop and use the spiritual gifts, talents, skills, and abilities God has given. They also lead through their examples of support for the church's ministries and leaders. As deacons develop a significant relationship with church families, they can be a natural communication channel for the church. Printed material and announcements can inform members about budgets, special events, and major changes taking place in the church. Deacons can also clarify and interpret church ministries to church families to enable understanding, and they can challenge and excite them to encourage support.

Deacons can help preserve church fellowship when conflict threatens. Deacons are sometimes called on to keep "the unity of the Spirit with the peace that binds us" (Eph. 4:3). A church committee was working on a major recommendation to be presented to the church. The committee learned that some members disagreed with the principles used to prepare the recommendation. The committee felt that it was appropriate to share with the deacons those principles and get feedback to help in decision making. The deacon chairman and others made clear that this was being taken to the deacons, not through the deacon body. The committee was not asking for formal approval or disapproval. They were seeking the insights of these elected leaders who had regular contact with the total congregation.

The committee received some significant and helpful insights both from those who agreed and those who disagreed. The deacons received information and understanding that enabled them to answer questions from members in the congregation and to encourage a spirit of fellowship.

Effective Christian leaders will do what needs to be done when it needs to be done. They will lead aggressively in the Christlike spirit of humble servants. This kind of leadership can enable persons to grow and the church to achieve its mission. That mission includes evangelizing to increase the number of believers, maturing persons in Christian faith, improving the quality of fellowship in the congregation, encouraging ministry inside and beyond the church, and focusing worship to glorify God.

After nearly forty years in management training and research for American Telephone and Telegraph Company, Robert Greenleaf wrote the book *Servant Leadership*. It is primarily addressed to leaders in businesses and institutions. He stated: "A fresh and critical look is being taken at the issues of power and authority, and people are beginning to learn, however haltingly, to relate to one another in less coercive and more creatively supportive ways. A new moral principle is emerging which holds that the only authority deserving one's allegiance is that which is freely and knowingly granted by the led to the leader in response to, and in proportion to, the clearly evident servant stature of the leader."[5] Of course, this principle is not really new but is a rediscovery of what Christ taught.

Some deacons will sense that God is directing them to apply their leadership skills to particular issues. John Woolman, an American Quaker, was this kind of leader. He determined to rid the Society of Friends (Quakers) of slavery through gentle but clear and persistent persuasion. Over a thirty-year period he repeatedly visited affluent, conservative Quaker slaveholders seeking to convince rather than coerce. Woolman primarily raised questions: "What does owning slaves do to you as a moral person? What kind of institution are you leaving for your children?" His patient work resulted in the elimination of slavery from the Society of Friends nearly one hundred years before the Civil War.[6] Deacons can be used by God to have this kind of influence.

When deacons model Christian leadership in their churches, they inevitably will find themselves serving as enabling leaders in their homes, on their jobs, and in community organizations. As these deacons are observed, some will be asked to assume important roles of leadership in their community, state, nation, and even in the international community. God uses deacons who model Christian character and leadership to accomplish his kingdom purposes in individual lives and in churches; in organizations such as schools, businesses, and civic clubs; in government; and in society in general. Churches should give these deacons encouragement and continuing prayerful support as they have broader opportunities to model the Christian life applied to leadership.

Conclusion

WHO A DEACON IS will be the foundation for what a deacon does. That is why this book has made such a strong emphasis on the high qualities that both God and the church expect of deacons. The congregation looks to its deacons to serve as models, as examples, of the quality of Christian living that God expects of all Christians. Only Jesus demonstrated the godly life completely. However, deacons should give evidence of progress toward that ideal in their present, continuing behavior.

The qualities of deacons who are serving as models in the church are grouped into four characteristics. Deacons will demonstrate growth toward mature faith, demonstrate Christian family life, demonstrate personal and public morality, and demonstrate a life accepted by God and the church.

The biblical qualifications for deacons suggest that growth toward mature faith will include growth in experiencing God's presence, in seeing from God's perspective, in integrating faith into life, and in demonstrating maturity. The evidence of such growth is in the lives that deacons live. Their wisdom and faith are seen as they carry out their ministry responsibilities. They have a reputation for "reflecting the glory of the Lord and . . . being transformed into the same image" (2 Cor. 3:18). Jesus said, "My Father is glorified by this: that you produce much fruit and prove to be My disciples" (John 15:8).

The deacon's family should not be expected to be perfect, but family members do have the opportunity to model

Christian family life. A deacon is to be the husband of one wife and to manage his children and family well. A deacon's wife is to demonstrate the same high standards as her husband. Healthy marriage and parent-child relationships provide an excellent opportunity for the deacon and his family to be an example in the church. The deacon's family can help other families see that an appropriate balance of meaningful family life, caring ministry, and active church involvement can be achieved.

Deacons should be persons of exemplary Christian character in their personal and public lives. The biblical qualifications suggest that deacons should have respected conduct, a controlled tongue, a Spirit-controlled body, and right priorities. A test of deacons' true character is their godly actions. They do not seek attention but give God the credit for any respect they receive. Since deacons are not to be double-tongued, they must be consistent in their speech and faithful in confidentiality if others are to consider them persons of integrity.

Since the Christian's body is the temple of the Holy Spirit, deacons are not to pay attention to or to be concerned about wine or anything else that would take the Spirit's place in controlling their bodies. Deacons will trust God rather than money and possessions as their source of security. Deacons who have right priorities will be released from anxiety, selfishness, and greed. They will desire God's kingdom, his rule, in their lives.

Christians live under the watchful eye of God and must not be afraid to have God see their thoughts and actions. Church members look to their deacons to follow Christ's example and thus be acceptable and pleasing to God. Church members cannot search the hearts or thoughts of deacons. They can evaluate only on the basis of words, attitudes, and actions. Of course, church members must be aware that the standard by which deacons are measured is the same used to measure themselves. The high expectations the church has of its deacons are no more than God expects of all Christians. The result of deacons being accepted by God and the church is not pride but confidence. Such confidence enables deacons to accomplish their assigned ministry. Thus, who deacons are becomes the foundation for what deacons do.

What deacons do is found in the very name itself—deacons are to be servants. They are to be ministers working alongside their pastor. As partners with the pastor, deacons have the privilege and opportunity to share in modeling ministry to the church. Deacons can be examples to the congregation as they carry out their duties of caring for families, proclaiming the gospel, and leading the church.

At times in church history, deacons have lost sight of their primary function of service in partnership with the pastor. One purpose of this book is to bring deacons back from being business managers functioning as a board of directors to a biblical understanding of their role. This book also seeks to correct the misinterpretation of Acts 6 by some writers that led to a wrong job description for deacons. Chapters 6 and 9 dealt with these issues. Deacons have a great heritage in ministry to persons. Sometimes in the past deacons have lost sight of their servant role, but today deacons are demonstrating a growing excitement as they have opportunity to share ministry with their pastor.

Churches turn to their deacons to help in caring for the needs of church members. Some churches have a deacon of the week to visit the sick and shut-ins and to be on call to work with the pastor in meeting other needs. Other churches have deacon teams to meet specific needs such as crisis ministry, new members, benevolence, and evangelism. Assigning each church family to a deacon is another approach to reduce the possibility that some members will be neglected. Deacons who build caring relationships through team ministry or family ministry will find it natural to minister in times of crisis. Church members will see deacons as familiar friends. Deacons can model care for families.

Another part of what deacons do is to proclaim the gospel to both nonbelievers and believers. Deacons who are concerned for others will be sensitive to appropriate opportunities to witness to non-Christians. This will be especially true as they build relationships with individuals and families through their deacon ministry. God can use those personal relationships as a basis for deacons giving a natural presentation of the gospel. Contact with families will also provide numerous opportunities to help Christians apply the gospel in their everyday lives. Sometimes God will lead deacons to speak out to challenge community attitudes, morals, and actions with biblical principles. Deacons need to be examples to the church and community in proclaiming the Word of God.

As servant leaders, deacons have the opportunity to demonstrate a quality of life and a quality of servant ministry that God would have for every Christian. Deacons who take their leadership role seriously can help their church accomplish God's purpose. Jesus is their model of servant leadership. Jesus made a clear contrast between secular and Christian leadership. Secular leadership measures status and prestige by the power to demand service from others. However, Jesus demonstrated that leadership is to be found in becoming a servant. Power is discovered in submission and service. When deacons serve well, those who receive their ministry will give them respect and will accept their leadership and influence.

The church and the world need servants who will care for individuals and families, proclaim the gospel to believers and nonbelievers, and provide Christian leadership. To be servants for the Lord as partners with him, deacons need the same qualities they demonstrated when they were first elected deacons—growth toward mature faith, Christian family life, personal and public morality, and ministry as partners. Such servants not only will reflect the likeness of Jesus but also will be models for the rest of the congregation and the world. The need for these characteristics to describe the lives of deacons cannot be overemphasized. "Those who have served well as deacons acquire a good standing for themselves, and great boldness in the faith that is in Christ Jesus" (1 Tim. 3:13).

Appendix
Word Study

This chart illustrates how *diakonos* and the related words in the
Greek New Testament are translated in the Holman Christian Standard Bible.

Diakonos
A noun used 30 times
identifying a table waiter,
a servant of a master,
a church leader.

Deacons (3)
Philippians 1:1
1 Timothy 3:8, 12

Servant(s) (19)
Matthew 20:26; 23:11
Mark 9:35; 10:43
John 2:5, 9; 12:26
Romans 16:1; 13:4 (twice);
    15:8
1 Corinthians 3:5
2 Corinthians 11:15
    (twice), 23
Ephesians 3:7; 6:21
Colossians 4:7
1 Timothy 4:6

Minister(s) (5)
2 Corinthians 3:6; 6:4
Colossians 1:7, 23, 25

Attendants (1)
Matthew 22:13

Promoter (1)
Galatians 2:17

Coworker (1)
1 Thessalonians 3:2

Diakonia
A noun used 34 times
describing the service
of love by those who
minister to others.

Ministry(ies) (22)
Acts 1:17; 6:4; 20:24;
    21:19
Romans 11:13
1 Corinthians 12:5
2 Corinthians 3:7, 8, 9
    (twice); 4:1; 5:18; 6:3;
    8:4; 9:1, 12; 11:8
Ephesians 4:12
Colossians 4:17
1 Timothy 1:12
2 Timothy 4:5, 11

Service, Serving (7)
Acts 1:25
Romans 12:7 (twice); 15:31
1 Corinthians 16:15
2 Corinthians 9:13
Revelation 2:19

Relief, Relief Mission (2)
Acts 11:29; 12:25

Distribution (1)
Acts 6:1

Server (1)
Hebrews 1:14

Tasks (1)
Luke 10:40

Diakoneo
A verb used 37 times
meaning to wait tables, serve
a master, care for, give
another a service of love.

Serve as deacons (2)
1 Timothy 3:10, 13

Serve(s, d), Serving (25)
Matthew 4:11; 8:15;
    20:28 (twice)
Mark 1:13, 31; 10:45 (twice)
Luke 4:39; 10:40; 12:37; 17:8;
    22:26, 27 (twice)
John 12:2, 26 (twice)
Romans 15:25
Philemon 13
Hebrews 6:10 (twice)
1 Peter 1:12; 4:10, 11

Minister(ed, ing) (3)
Matthew 27:55
Mark 15:41
2 Timothy 1:18

Administered (2)
2 Corinthians 8:19, 20

Wait on (1)
Acts 6:2

Help (1)
Matthew 25:44

Assisted (1)
Acts 19:22

Supporting (1)
Luke 8:3

Produced (1)
2 Corinthians 3:3

Appendix
Word Study

This chart illustrates how *diakonos* and the related words in the Greek New Testament are translated in the King James Version.

Diakonos	*Diakonia*	*Diakoneo*
A noun used 30 times identifying a table waiter, a servant of a master, a church leader.	A noun used 34 times describing the service of love by those who minister to others.	A verb used 37 times meaning to wait tables, serve a master, care for, give another a service of love.

Deacons (3)
Philippians 1:1
1 Timothy 3:8, 12

Minister(s) (20)
Matthew 20:26
Mark 10:43
Romans 13:4 (twice); 15:8
1 Corinthians 3:5
2 Corinthians 3:6; 6:4;
   11:15 (twice), 23
Galatians 2:17
Ephesians 3:7; 6:21
Colossians 1:7, 23, 25;
   4:7
1 Thessalonians 3:2
1 Timothy 4:6

Servant(s) (7)
Matthew 22:13; 23:11
Mark 9:35
John 2:5, 9; 12:26
Romans 16:1

Ministry(ies) (16)
Acts 1:17, 25; 6:4;
   12:25; 20:24; 21:19
Romans 12:7
1 Corinthians 16:15
2 Corinthians 4:1; 5:18; 6:3
Ephesians 4:12
Colossians 4:17
1 Timothy 1:12
2 Timothy 4:5, 11

Ministration (6)
Acts 6:1
2 Corinthians 3:7, 8,
   9 (twice); 9:13

Service, Serving (4)
Luke 10:40
Romans 15:31
2 Corinthians 11:8
Revelation 2:19

Minister(ing) (4)
Romans 12:7
2 Corinthians 8:4; 9:1
Hebrews 1:14

Administration (2)
1 Corinthians 12:5
2 Corinthians 9:12

Office (1)
Romans 11:13

Relief (1)
Acts 11:29

Use(d) the office of a deacon (2)
1 Timothy 3:10, 13

Minister(ed, ing) (23)
Matthew 4:11; 8:15;
   20:28 (twice);
   25:44; 27:55
Mark 1:13, 31; 10:45
   (twice); 15:41
Luke 4:39; 8:3
Acts 19:22
Romans 15:25
2 Corinthians 3:3
2 Timothy 1:18
Philemon 13
Hebrews 6:10 (twice)
1 Peter 1:12; 4:10, 11

Serve(d, th) (10)
Luke 10:40; 12:37; 17:8;
   22:26, 27 (twice)
John 12:2, 26 (twice)
Acts 6:2

Administered (2)
2 Corinthians 8:19, 20

Notes

Chapter 1

1. Gaines S. Dobbins, "The Meaning of Ordination," *Church Administration*, December 1960.

2. H. H. Hobbs, "Ordination," *Encyclopedia of Southern Baptists* (Nashville: Broadman, 1958), 2:1057.

3. Charles W. Deweese, *The Emerging Role of Deacons* (Nashville: Broadman, 1979), 79–82.

Chapter 2

1. Richard J. Foster, *Celebration of Discipline: The Path to Spiritual Growth* (New York: Harper & Row, 1978), 15.

2. Elizabeth O'Connor, *Search for Silence* (Waco: Word, 1972), 72.

3. Foster, 30.

4. Samuel M. Shoemaker, *With the Holy Spirit and with Fire* (Waco: Word, 1960), 31.

5. Roy Edgemon and Barry Sneed, *Jesus by Heart: God Can Transform You to Be Like Jesus* (Nashville: LifeWay Press, 1999), 10.

6. Fred L. Fisher, *Falling Walls: The Doctrine of Reconciliation* (Nashville: Convention, 1971), 62–63.

7. C. Gene Wilkes, *My Identity in Christ* (Nashville: LifeWay Press, 1999), 61–62.

8. Thomas Merton, *Contemplative Prayer* (Garden City, NY: Doubleday, 1969), 37.

9. T. B. Maston, *Why Live the Christian Life?* (Nashville: Broadman, 1974), 138.

Chapter 3

1. See Deweese, 15, 30, 38, 49, 57–59.

Chapter 4

1. Dennis L. Brewer, "Uncle Jeems and Brother Fred," *The Deacon*, January 1979, 44.

Chapter 6

1. Ernest E. Mosley, *Called to Joy: A Design for Pastoral Ministries* (Nashville: Convention, 1973), 25.

2. The primary source of the historical information is Deweese, *The Emerging Role of Deacons.*

3. R. B. C. Howell, *The Deaconship* (Philadelphia: American Baptist Publication Society, 1846), 12.

4. Ibid., 122–23.

5. Ibid., 18.

6. P. E. Burroughs, *Honoring the Deaconship* (Nashville: Sunday School Board, 1929), 17.

7. Ibid., 21.

8. Robert E. Naylor, *The Baptist Deacon* (Nashville: Broadman, 1955), 3.

9. Ibid., 20–21, 88ff.

10. Foshee, *The Ministry of the Deacon* (Nashville: Convention, 1968), 35–36.

Chapter 7

1. Robert Sheffield, compiler, *Handbook for Planning Deacon Ministry* (Nashville: LifeWay Press, 1999), 49.

2. Deweese, 13.

3. J. T. Henderson, *The Office of Deacon* (Knoxville: n.p., 1928), 89–90.

4. From *The Deacon*, July 1975, 32.

5. Robert W. Bailey, "From Limited Ministry to Family Ministry Plan," *The Deacon*, January 1978, 36.

6. C. W. Brister, *Take Care* (Nashville: Broadman, 1978), 113.

7. Alvin Toffler, *Future Shock* (New York: Bantam, 1970), 371.

8. Sidney M. Jourard, *The Transparent Self* (New York: D. Van Nostrand, 1971), 37–39.

Chapter 8

1. William Fay and Ralph Hodge, *Share Jesus Without Fear* (Nashville: LifeWay Press, 1997), 12.

2. Howard J. Clinebell Jr., *The People Dynamic* (New York: Harper & Row, 1972), 40.

3. Bruce Larson, *No Longer Strangers* (Waco: Word, 1971), 52.

Chapter 9

1. C. Gene Wilkes, *Jesus on Leadership* (Wheaton: Tyndale, 1998), 130–131.

2. Wallace Denton, "A Man for All Seasons—the Baptist Deacon," *The Deacon*, July 1979, 38.

3. Howard B. Foshee, *The Ministry of the Deacon* (Nashville: Convention, 1968), 33.

4. Richard J. Foster, *Celebration of Discipline* (New York: Harper & Row, 1978), 115.

5. Robert K. Greenleaf, *Servant Leadership: A Journey into the Nature of Legitimate Power and Greatness* (New York: Paulist, 1977), 9–10.

6. Ibid., 29–30.

About the Author

HENRY WEBB is director of Church Leadership Publishing for LifeWay Church Resources, a division of LifeWay Christian Resources. He has served as pastor of Kalihi Baptist Church, Honolulu, Hawaii; as editor of *The Deacon* magazine; and as LifeWay's national deacon consultant. He received the doctor of ministry degree from Golden Gate Baptist Theological Seminary.